T0029331

ESL GAMES FOR THE CLASSROOM

ESL
Games
for the
Classroom

**101 Interactive Activities to Engage
Your Students with Minimal Prep**

Michael DiGiacomo

**ZEPHYROS
PRESS**

Copyright © 2018 by Zephyros Press, Emeryville, California

No part of this publication may be reproduced, stored in a retrieval system, or transmitted in any form or by any means, electronic, mechanical, photocopying, recording, scanning, or otherwise, except as permitted under Sections 107 or 108 of the 1976 United States Copyright Act, without the prior written permission of the Publisher. Requests to the Publisher for permission should be addressed to the Permissions Department, Zephyros Press, 6005 Shellmound Street, Suite 175, Emeryville, CA 94608.

Limit of Liability/Disclaimer of Warranty: The Publisher and the author make no representations or warranties with respect to the accuracy or completeness of the contents of this work and specifically disclaim all warranties, including without limitation warranties of fitness for a particular purpose. No warranty may be created or extended by sales or promotional materials. The advice and strategies contained herein may not be suitable for every situation. This work is sold with the understanding that the Publisher is not engaged in rendering medical, legal, or other professional advice or services. If professional assistance is required, the services of a competent professional person should be sought. Neither the Publisher nor the author shall be liable for damages arising herefrom. The fact that an individual, organization, or website is referred to in this work as a citation and/or potential source of further information does not mean that the author or the Publisher endorses the information the individual, organization, or website may provide or recommendations they/it may make. Further, readers should be aware that Internet websites listed in this work may have changed or disappeared between when this work was written and when it is read.

For general information on our other products and services or to obtain technical support, please contact our Customer Care Department within the U.S. at (866) 744-2665, or outside the U.S. at (510) 253-0500.

Zephyros Press publishes its books in a variety of electronic and print formats. Some content that appears in print may not be available in electronic books, and vice versa.

TRADEMARKS: Zephyros Press and the Zephyros Press logo are trademarks or registered trademarks of Callisto Media Inc. and/or its affiliates, in the United States and other countries, and may not be used without written permission. All other trademarks are the property of their respective owners. Zephyros Press is not associated with any product or vendor mentioned in this book.

Cover background illustration © Shutterstock.com/topform

Cover Designer: William D. Mack
Interior Designer: Meg Woodcheke
Editor: Brian Hurley
Production Editor: Andrew Yackira

ISBN: Print 978-1-64152-109-3 | eBook 978-1-64152-110-9

This book is inspired by and dedicated to
all of the students I have worked with
over the years.

Contents

Introduction

THE IMPORTANCE OF PLAY

I'm a native New Yorker who has been helping people learn English since 1994. Since the beginning of my career teaching English as a second language (ESL) and English as a foreign language (EFL) at a private, adult language school in Sendai, Japan, games like the ones in this book have played an important role in my classes.

A fundamental concept of language is that it contains both input (reading and listening) and output (speaking and writing). In order for second-language learning to successfully take place, students need practice on the output side of the equation, particularly in speaking. That's where games come in. Second-language learners, especially at the beginner and intermediate levels, tend to be extremely hesitant about speaking. This is a generalization, I know, and it varies depending on a student's cultural background and the level of English they have already mastered. But games are a great way to get your students talking.

First of all, games and activities like these are fun, and having fun is an essential ingredient of learning a language. Have fun while learning? Yes, you can. Many students may come from backgrounds where the classroom is a serious place for learning. They may be used to a more passive learning experience in which the teacher lectures and the students quietly absorb. In some countries, students' language-learning experience is focused on reading, writing, and translating, with little or no opportunity for speaking. In Japan, for example, students learn English in both junior and senior high school, yet in those six years, they have little opportunity to converse, so they are often reluctant to speak. Fun activities, like games, can help such students feel more at ease about using the language they have studied.

As you probably know from your own second-language learning experience, it's not easy to open your mouth and produce vocabulary or a particular pattern of grammar for the first time. It's nerve-racking for students, so having fun is a great way to break that tension in the classroom. Using entertaining games and activities can lower your students' affective barriers and make learning more meaningful. Many adult students have studied English at school, and that experience leads them to approach learning English as an academic subject rather a communication tool. Games can break those old stereotypes and help students enjoy English.

I wrote this book for you because it's the book that was missing on my shelf when I started teaching. First of all, most of the ESL activity books out there are based on British English, and I am not particularly fond of exercises and activities that talk about lorry drivers (truck drivers), flatmates (roommates), and trolleys (shopping carts). I feel it's time we American teachers have a classroom resource written in a language we use every day.

Second, every teacher needs a go-to book—a resource you can count on for just the right activity to warm up the class, round out a lesson, or drill a particular grammar or vocabulary point. Many of the games in this book can also be adapted to different levels, so they give you a lot of flexibility. I think you're going to love the mileage you get from these exercises, for in addition to using them in their current format, you can easily turn them into a launchpad for your own creative activities.

HOW TO USE THIS BOOK

The best kinds of games and activities are those your students can quickly grasp with minimal explanation. You'll find 101 of these in this book. The games here are easy, both for the teacher to execute and for the students to play. The other factor that makes for a good game is insignificant prep time. Teachers already have a lot to do when planning their lessons, so the need to spend a lot of time preparing for a 10-minute exercise just isn't worth it. Therefore, think of this book as your deli of classroom treats. All of the soups, salads, and sandwiches you could want are right here.

The games in this book are ideal for large classes, but most activities can work equally well for pairs or small groups. The benefit of fewer participants is to give students more time speaking and listening and less time "waiting for my turn." Nothing makes students more bored than a class activity requiring them to wait long periods before speaking. I've seen classes where the teacher goes around the class, asking students one by one, "How was your weekend?" Oh, how sorry I feel for the 15th student in the class patiently waiting to speak. By breaking your class down into smaller groups, all students can experience the maximum amount of participation and the minimum amount of boredom.

For many of these games, the teacher can simply model the activity with one or two students to demonstrate how the game works. Modeling is a best friend of the ESL classroom because it provides the students with a clear example of what to do. Students at lower levels in particular can get totally lost in a game's explanation, so modeling shows them what they need to achieve in a comprehensible way.

In the traditional classroom, the teacher takes the role of game show host or dealer while the students are players. However, in this book, the format is different. The activities here are student centered and teacher guided, meaning that in most of the activities, the students do most of the work. Working in groups, students act as the host or dealer and then have the chance to switch roles and become a player. This enables the teacher to monitor the class and facilitate the activities as needed.

Many of the games in this book can be used by teachers in private lessons as well. Since many of the activities here are based on pair work, you can serve as the partner for your one-to-one student. Quite often, private lessons can fall into free-conversation sessions (without direction for learning) or just stick to the usual humdrum routine of lessons (without inspiration). It can be a challenge for the one-to-one teacher to bring the feeling of fun and excitement characteristic of group classes to these lessons. Simply due to the nature of the beast, groups are more social and can produce more of a party atmosphere than a one-to-one class. Introducing these games will therefore help teachers instill their private lessons with some creative flair.

So how to choose which game to play? All the games are organized according to the primary type of skill they practice, such as grammar, vocabulary, speaking, listening, and so on. Therefore, each chapter highlights a skill, and the games it presents are arranged by difficulty, ranging from beginner (Level 1) to advanced (Level 5). The games in this book have all been rated on a scale of 1 to 5, per the following chart.

LEVEL 1	Beginner
LEVEL 2	False beginner and lower intermediate
LEVEL 3	Intermediate
LEVEL 4	Upper intermediate and pre-advanced
LEVEL 5	Advanced

While browsing each chapter, you'll notice that games also list group size, materials, and time required, so you can pick a game suitable to those criteria, too, if you like. Once you have begun to familiarize yourself with the format, be sure to flip to the Choose a Game chart at the end, which lists every game in the book. Scan this chart to compare the games at a glance and help choose the perfect activity for any situation.

Teacher Survival Guide

TIPS FOR GREAT GAMES

I invite you to think of the games and activities in this book as a starting point, similar to a recipe for soup. When making soup, you adjust the ingredients and seasonings to suit your taste, and in teaching English, you'll probably want to adjust the activities to suit your students and class dynamic. Here are some tips to help you do that.

Have fun. You know the old line about catching more flies with honey, right? Your students will make more progress when they are learning in a fun, playful environment than in a serious, formal one. They probably had serious lessons when they were in high school or college, and that's why they are in your class now!

Get to know your students. The ESL class becomes like an extended family. It's a supportive environment where mistakes are brushed off as simply part of the learning process.

Help students out of their comfort zone. Some of the games and activities here have students leading the game in turns. Doing this encourages all students to actively participate.

Be flexible. The group size indicated in each game is an example. You may feel an activity works better in pairs or with a bigger group. You know your students best, so go for it.

Repetition is good! You may think, for example, that you have practiced the second conditional enough, but that doesn't mean your students have had enough opportunity to use it. Covering a topic one more time never hurts.

Cross-pollinate. Even though many of the games in this book have a particular language point focus, you can use them as stand-alone speaking and listening activities, regardless of what grammar lesson you may have covered that week. The end goal of any ESL program is that the students can communicate in English.

Use reality! The best materials for students come from their own world, not the textbook. If your students are fans of your local sports team, use those players as examples. Incorporate local attractions, shops, and other people they know (like your school director) as examples as much as possible.

Take yourself out of the mix. Most of the games here don't require the teacher's involvement aside from getting the game off the ground. This is because sometimes you need to let go of the baby's hand so they can try to walk by themselves. Your students need to gain confidence in English by using the language without you!

Be supportive when they fall down. Error correction is a topic that could fill its own book, but keep in mind you don't need to correct every error you hear. Focus on helping the students when they get lost using the target language during a game.

Avoid total meltdown! It's always a good idea to demonstrate any activity or game before handing it off to the students.

Never tell the students the rules before the game; just model the activity. Phrases like "Okay, guys, next up we are going to play a game where you need to guess the opposite of the adjective your partner says"—yikes! The explanation is a lesson in itself. Instead, demonstrate it, like "Up? Down. Black? White."

Have a plan B. Sometimes the activity may not be suitable for your class, or the setup may not have been adequate for the students to play the game as you intended. It's always a good idea to have a backup activity prepared.

COMMON SETBACKS
(AND HOW TO DEAL WITH THEM)

Sometimes things don't go as planned. That's life, right? Well, here are some tips to help you out during those moments and to hopefully avoid them in the first place.

Prepare your students! One of the key reasons a game or activity fails is because the students have not had enough practice or do not know the language point well enough to play the game successfully.

Selective pairing. You know who the quiet ones and the talkative ones are. Pair up or group your students so that there is a good balance in each group.

Dominance. Some strong personalities in the class may try to dominate an activity. This is why I avoid games and activities that are teacher led and involve the whole class. If you have such overbearing students, don't provide them with an environment that leads to an opportunity to take over.

Helping shy learners. Shy students in general work better in small groups or pair activities as opposed to having to make speeches in front of the class.

Avoid taboo topics. Even though we Americans like to debate the hottest news topics among our friends and families (women's rights, racism, politics, etc.), those may be very uncomfortable for students because of their cultural backgrounds. Class activities focusing on those topics will certainly fail.

Learn about your students' cultures. For example, Muslim women can't touch men (by shaking hands, for example), so any activity that involves any potential physical contact should be avoided.

Mix nationalities. When forming groups, encourage students of different nationalities to interact as much as possible. This will naturally force the students to use only English.

Know their personalities. Let's face it, everyone in the class won't always get along. Games and activities will work better if you keep adversaries apart.

Silence is not golden. If you have students working in groups, and one group finishes before the others, be prepared with an additional task or activity to keep those students occupied while they are waiting for the rest of the class.

Fair pairing. If you have an odd number of students and you need to be a partner, switch pairs often so that all of the students can have the chance to chat one-on-one with the teacher. Otherwise, opt for pairs plus one group of three.

Independence for all. Students tend to rely on the teacher too much, so help your students wean themselves off you. When my students ask me a question, my two favorite answers are "I don't know; what do you think?" and "I don't know; ask Giuseppe."

Know the distracters. Sometimes students will go off topic either intentionally or organically. Monitor the student groups to keep them focused on the task at hand.

ONE-TO-ONE

If you teach private lessons, you're in luck. Many of the games and activities in this book can easily be adapted for one-to-one teaching or a small class. In a private lesson, you become the partner, and if your class is small, you can partner up with the group. The best thing to keep in mind in a private lesson is to let your student dominate the conversation. I often have to tell myself, "Wait," so that my student has the chance to formulate what to say.

DIGITAL CLASSROOMS

Are you an online teacher? If so, you can easily use the games and activities in this book with your online classes. The website Quizlet.com can turn the cards from the activities in this book into online flashcards that you can easily share with your students. I also recommend the video chat site Zoom.us. Not only does it allow you to share a chat window, but it also gives you the opportunity to share any open window on your computer with the other person. For the games in this book that involve pictures or illustrations, you can use Zoom to show that image to the student(s).

Speaking Games

Reply Relay

Additional Skills: Speaking (questions), Listening

LEVEL:
1 to 3

GROUP:
WHOLE
CLASS

5 to 10
MINUTES

MATERIALS & PREP WORK

Prepare two sets of cards. One set has questions, like "Where is the train station?" "How much are the apples?" "What time does the movie start?" and "How many cats live in this city?" The other set contains the answers. Make enough so that each student will have two cards from either one set or the other.

THE GAME

The object of the game is for students to find matching answers to the questions on their cards.

HOW TO PLAY

Divide your class in half, then give one half two question cards each and the other half two answer cards each. The goal is for the students with the question cards to get rid of them. To do this, they must find the person who responds with the matching answer. The rule is that the students are allowed to say only what is written on their cards. The first student to get rid of his or her question cards is the winner. To balance out the activity, do it a second time, switching the groups that held the answers and questions.

WHAT TO LOOK FOR

Make sure the students are working quickly and speaking only the words on their cards.

Make sure you write the cards so that there is only one matching answer per question.

Giving Directions

Additional Skills: Speaking (asking for/ giving directions, discussing location, using prepositions), Listening

LEVEL:
1 to 3

GROUP:
2

10 to 15
MINUTES

MATERIALS & PREP WORK

Prepare a map of your town, your neighborhood, or a fictitious location. The map should cover at least a five-block area, and each block should contain street names and several buildings or places labeled by their names—for example, post office, bank, bookstore, café, supermarket, and parking lot. Then write each place name on a card. You will need one map and one set of cards for each pair of students.

THE GAME

The object of the game is for students to both give and listen to directions from one point on a map to another.

HOW TO PLAY

Model the game by identifying the starting point and then giving directions to a mystery destination. For example, tell the students, "I'm at the bank. I go straight on Main Street and turn left on Broadway. I stop at the corner of Broadway and Smith Street. Where am I?" Once the students catch on, have them play with their partners. One person draws two cards and reads aloud the first place name: "I'm at [place]." He or she then gives directions to the place on the second card without showing or saying what is written on it, and the partner has to name the destination. At the end of the first round, the second student takes two cards and assumes the role of the direction giver.

WHAT TO LOOK FOR

Make sure that the student giving the directions is using the target language and that the games are progressing correctly.

For a variation, after the first round, let the second student start at the first student's destination and draw just one card as the mystery location.

Tongue Twister Chain

Additional Skills: Speaking (enunciation), Listening

LEVEL:
1 to 5

GROUP:
4 or 5

10 to 15 MINUTES

MATERIALS & PREP WORK

Prepare a list of tongue twisters.

THE GAME

The purpose of this game is for groups of students to practice saying tongue twisters one person and one word at a time.

HOW TO PLAY

Write a tongue twister on the board—for example, "She sells seashells by the seashore." Then demonstrate the activity using one of the groups. Let's say the group has four students. The game will go as follows: S1: "She"; S2: "sells"; S3: "seashells"; S4: "by"; S1: "the"; S2: "seashore." Then, have them switch who goes first until each person in the group has had a turn starting the sentence.

WHAT TO LOOK FOR

You'll know it's working when the groups are able to smoothly recite the tongue twister.

Feel free to substitute another tongue twister or do several in order.

The Smartest Student

4

LEVEL:
2 to 4

GROUP:
3 or 4

10 to 15
MINUTES

Additional Skills: Speaking
(intonation, pronunciation)

MATERIALS & PREP WORK

None.

THE GAME

This game requires students to determine and discuss how the meaning of a sentence changes depending on which word is stressed.

HOW TO PLAY

We tend to stress certain words in a sentence for meaning. A basic example is "You look nice." If we stress *you*, it emphasizes the person. If we stress *look*, it emphasizes that you look nice, meaning you might appear nice (but aren't truly so). Write the following sentence on the board: "I think he is really the smartest student I have ever seen in this class." The students are to practice speaking that sentence with their partners, placing stress on each word of the sentence one at a time. Then, they need to discuss how the meaning shifts with the change of stress, as described above.

WHAT TO LOOK FOR

Lower-level students may need some help understanding how to stress different words in the sentence.

Feel free to substitute your own key sentence depending on the abilities of your class. Keep in mind, the longer the sentence, the more effective the activity.

Chain Story

Additional Skills: Speaking, Listening, Grammar

LEVEL:
2 to 4

GROUP:
4

10 to 15
MINUTES

MATERIALS & PREP WORK

None.

THE GAME

The object of this game is to invent a story on the spot. In this improvisation activity, one student begins the story, then each student has a turn to continue it.

HOW TO PLAY

Write the following on the board: "1. Who? This is the story of a man/a woman named _____."
Below this question and answer, write in a column, "2. Where?" "3. When?" and "4. What?" Have students sit in groups of four, and explain that they're going to tell a story beginning with the sentence on the board. Assign one student to be the "anchor." This student must decide the name of the story's main character and begin telling the story using

the sentence above. The other students in turn must continue the story, one sentence at a time, by creating sentences that answer the questions on the board: Where, when, and what? Once they have completed this, the story will include all key elements. An example might look like this: "This is the story of a man named Jack. Jack lives in Brooklyn. Yesterday, Jack went to work. Jack works at a pizza shop." If you and your students like, the story can continue from there.

WHAT TO LOOK FOR

You'll know it's working when the students are speaking in turns to continue the story based on the previous person's contribution.

You may want lower-level students to write the story down to reinforce their use of language or to help them build the story. For higher-level students, you might tell them to concentrate on a particular tense, such as placing the story primarily in the future.

How Was Your Weekend?

6

★

LEVEL:
2 to 4

GROUP:
2

🕐

10
MINUTES

Additional Skills: Speaking
(reported speech), Listening

MATERIALS & PREP WORK

None.

THE GAME

The object of the game is to create a mixer where students talk about their weekend with one partner and then report the same information to another using the language of reported speech.

HOW TO PLAY

This is a mixer activity that starts by having your students stand up and work in pairs. On the board, write the key question, "What did you do last weekend?" (If you choose to do this on a weekday later in the week than Monday, change the question to "What did you do yesterday?") The students have to ask and answer the question with their partners. After five minutes, stop the pairs and ask them to change partners. Now, using the various forms of reported speech, the students need to tell their new partners what their first partners did over the weekend.

WHAT TO LOOK FOR

Make sure the pairs are on task, especially in the second half of the activity, when they need to report the activities of their first partners—not their own.

For lower levels, write the key reported speech patterns on the board—for example, "Kim said that _____," "Kim told me _____," and so on. For higher-level classes, teach the students how to use the colloquial expression "was like" before the activity.

Magazine Photos

Additional Skills: Speaking (describing appearance), Listening

LEVEL:
2 to 4

GROUP:
5 or 6

10 to 15
MINUTES

MATERIALS & PREP WORK

Prepare 15 to 20 magazine photos of people. These can include a mix of famous and nonfamous individuals.

THE GAME

The object of this game is for students to be able to accurately describe the appearance of someone as well as identify a person being described.

HOW TO PLAY

To model this activity, write on the board the key sentences, "I'm trying to find one of my friends. Can you help me?" Then describe the appearance of one of the students in your class—for example,

"My friend has short brown hair and dark eyes. She is in her mid-20s," and so on. Once the students get the idea, have them work in their groups. Place 15 to 20 different pictures on a table. One student in each group chooses a photo (without pointing it out) and describes the person shown. The other students need to look at the pictures and guess which person their classmate is describing.

WHAT TO LOOK FOR

The students should describe the physical appearance of the person before referring to what they're wearing.

You might also use a photo of an audience at a concert or a sporting event. If you have a projector in the classroom, you can show that picture to the class and let them use it for this activity.

Who Are We Talking About?

8

LEVEL:
2 to 4

GROUP:
2

15 to 20
MINUTES

Additional Skills: Speaking (describing appearance), Listening

MATERIALS & PREP WORK

Prepare a handout with facial-characteristic vocabulary, such as hair color, hairstyle (long, short, wavy, etc.), eye color, nose size, lip size, and face shape.

THE GAME

The object of the game is for students to identify which of their classmates is being described.

HOW TO PLAY

Give a handout to each student, and have each pair of students sit back-to-back. Students need to ask their partners to describe their appearance. For example, one student says, "Tell me about your hair." The partner replies, "I have shoulder-length brown hair." The first student continues, "Is your hair straight or wavy?" and so on. The students must write down the responses with as much detail as possible and then switch roles. When the pairs have finished, collect the papers, shuffle them, and hand them out again to the class. Students now read the description in front of them and try to guess which classmate is being described.

WHAT TO LOOK FOR

You'll know this is working when the pairs have pretty detailed descriptions of their partners. Make sure they are writing the descriptions in sentences and not just jotting down words.

Higher-level students may not need a handout with the key vocabulary.

Two Numbers, Two Words

9

LEVEL:
2 to 5

GROUP:
2 or 3

10 to 15 MINUTES

Additional Skills: Speaking (questions), Listening

MATERIALS & PREP WORK
None.

THE GAME
In this game, students must ask yes-or-no questions to find out the meaning of two numbers and two words written by their partners.

HOW TO PLAY
On a piece of paper, students write down two numbers and two words that are somehow connected to their life. An example of a number might be an important year (date of graduation,

arrival in the city, etc.), number of children, or age. An example of a word could be a favorite food or animal. The students then exchange the paper with their partners, and the partners try to guess what the numbers and words mean by asking questions. A key requirement is that students ask only yes-or-no questions and the student responding reply only with yes or no as well.

WHAT TO LOOK FOR

Make sure the students are not asking questions that call for answers beyond a simple yes or no.

For lower-level students, you could permit them to ask and answer *who, what, where, when,* and *why* questions as well.

The Fastest Lyrics

10

Additional Skills: Speaking (speed, pronunciation)

LEVEL:
2 to 5

GROUP:
2

10 to 15
MINUTES

MATERIALS & PREP WORK

Prepare a worksheet with the lyrics of a well-known song, such as "Yesterday" by the Beatles or "Living on a Prayer" by Bon Jovi.

THE GAME

The object of the game is for pairs of students to practice smooth, easy speech by reading song lyrics as fast and accurately as possible.

HOW TO PLAY

Hand out a copy of the lyrics to each student, play the song (you can find most songs on YouTube), and let the students get familiar with it. Then, have each pair of students read the song through together. Each member of the pair then takes a turn reading one line from the lyrics at a time. The team that can get through the entire song the fastest is the winner.

WHAT TO LOOK FOR

Help the students with reductions or linking sounds as appropriate and as needed.

For more talkative or bolder students, you can ask them to speed-sing the song (if they are already familiar with it). For a bigger challenge, avoid songs with repetitive phrases.

A Dark and Stormy Night

11

LEVEL:
2 to 5

GROUP:
3 or 4

10 to 15
MINUTES

Additional Skills: Speaking, Listening, Grammar, Vocabulary

MATERIALS & PREP WORK

Write down the first line of each of several famous novels or songs, one for each group of students. Some examples are "It was a dark and stormy night"; "Hello, darkness, my old friend"; "Once upon a time there was . . ."; "Who's there?" and so on.

THE GAME

The goal of this game is for students to tell (or write) a story that begins with a typical or classic line from a famous story or song. Students are meant to use this first line as the starting point and move on from there. Lower-level classes can write the story down, but this can be an oral exercise for higher levels.

HOW TO PLAY

You will need to demonstrate this activity for the whole class first. Tell the students that you are going to create a story together. Elicit a character, name, age, and place from the class. Let's say the class makes up a character named Bob who is 20 years old and lives in New York City. Then, write on the board, "It was a dark and stormy night." Ask the class what happens next: "What did Bob do?" or "What happened to Bob?" One student answers, "Bob was walking home from work." You might then ask, "Okay, and how was he feeling?" Another student might respond, "He was hungry." Continue like this until the students catch on what to do. Then, hand each group another opening line. Tell the students that just like the example with Bob, they need to take that opening line and tell the story.

WHAT TO LOOK FOR

You'll know it's working when the students are smoothly taking turns to create the story in their groups.

You can either give a different first line to each group or stick to the same first line for all the groups. At the end of the activity, have the groups read or tell their stories to the rest of the class.

12

Did You Say . . . ?

Additional Skills: Speaking (pronunciation of minimal pairs), Listening

LEVEL:
2 to 5

GROUP:
3 or 4

10 to 15
MINUTES

MATERIALS & PREP WORK

Prepare cards on which you write two sentences containing a minimal pair—for example, "Did you remember to count the (votes/boats)?" and "I'm not happy with those (votes/boats)." Use a different minimal pair for each card, and make enough cards to give a different one to each student in the class.

THE GAME

In this game, students read aloud a sentence to their group members, who write down the words they hear with the goal of correctly matching the dictated sentence.

HOW TO PLAY

Hand out the cards and ask the students to circle one of the words in their minimal pair to read. Then, have one student read his or her chosen sentences to the others in the group. They must write down what the first student said and then check with each other to see if they wrote down the same thing. Once the group has a consensus, the first student shows the group which minimal-pair word was circled. Play then continues with the next student.

WHAT TO LOOK FOR

The students should be working together toward a group consensus—they need to achieve this for the game to continue.

For lower-level classes, include just one sentence per card.

13

Dead Guy in the Hat

Additional Skills: Speaking (question formation), Grammar

LEVEL:
3 to 5

GROUP:
WHOLE
CLASS

⏰
20 to 30
MINUTES

MATERIALS & PREP WORK

Prepare two or three small pieces of blank paper for each student. Or have each student tear a page from their notebook and tear it into two or three pieces.

THE GAME

The object of the game is for the students to guess the names of famous—but not living—people by asking yes-or-no questions.

HOW TO PLAY

Hand out the pieces of paper or ask the students to rip pages from their notebooks. The students need to come up with the names of famous but not living people. These should be world-famous musicians, artists, politicians, and so on, such as Einstein, Beethoven, and Picasso. (It's best to avoid individuals celebrated in one's own county. While Ben Franklin is famous, for example, he may be less familiar to those from outside the United States.)

Students write one name per piece of paper and then fold the paper in half. They must not show their classmates these names. Collect all of the pieces of paper in a hat (or box) and mix them up. Elect one person to be the moderator. The moderator can then draw one name without showing it to the class. Then, the students must ask the moderator only yes-or-no questions in an effort to guess the name of the person—for example, "Is it a man?" "Is it a musician?" "Is he from China?" and so on. The student who guesses the name of the celebrity wins the round, and the next name can be drawn.

WHAT TO LOOK FOR

You'll know the game is working when the students are actively asking questions and all the students are participating.

Instead of making the students come up with the list of celebrity names, you can do this in advance of the class yourself. If you have a group of students of one nationality, provide a list of famous people from their country.

The Perfect
New Roommate

14

★
LEVEL:
3 to 5

GROUP:
WHOLE
CLASS

🕐
20 to 25
MINUTES

Additional Skills: Speaking, Vocabulary

MATERIALS & PREP WORK

Prepare "personality cards" with four or five
lifestyle/personality traits on each card—for
example, "I'm a doctor. I like skiing and eating out.
I don't like cats or dogs, but I have a pet bird."
Make enough cards to give one to each student.

THE GAME

The object of the game is for the students to walk
around the room and find someone who would be
a perfect match for their roommate search.

HOW TO PLAY

This is like a speed-dating event. Hand out the cards and tell the students they need to assume the role as indicated there. This becomes their new personality. Then ask the students to find a partner. They will have two to three minutes to chat up that partner and decide if they want them for a roommate or not, based on a personality and lifestyle match. Then call time, and the students need to chat up another partner. After several rounds, the students report if they have found the perfect roommate or not.

WHAT TO LOOK FOR

Make sure the students are sticking to their role as described on the card as they look for a roommate.

> Try to be creative when preparing the cards. For example, make half of the class dog lovers and the other half cat lovers.

Just One of the Actors

LEVEL:
3 to 5

GROUP:
2

🕐
10 to 15
MINUTES

Additional Skills: Speaking, Listening

MATERIALS & PREP WORK

Prepare a short video clip and transcript from a TV sitcom, like *Seinfeld* or *Friends*. It should be a short scene with just two people speaking, perhaps 10 to 16 lines (5 to 8 lines each). Transcripts can be readily found online.

THE GAME

In this activity, students aim to practice the speed and timing of native speakers by speaking the lines from a short scene of a TV program along with the video.

HOW TO PLAY

Hand out a copy of the script (easily found online). Watch the scene once or twice, then read through the scene with the class. Go over any reductions or linking sounds with the group. Then have the students work in pairs to practice role-playing the scene. When they feel ready, students can come up to the front of the class and take turns speaking the lines of the second person in the scene along with the video clip.

WHAT TO LOOK FOR

You may want to help students with the phrasing and intonation as well as any reductions.

I suggest having your students repeat the second character's speech because the first character can provide the student with timing cues for speaking the lines. For more advanced students, have the pairs speak the lines of both characters.

Survivor

Additional Skills: Speaking, Listening

LEVEL:
3 to 5

GROUP:
3 or 4

15 to 20
MINUTES

MATERIALS & PREP WORK

None.

THE GAME

In this game, students pick eight items they would choose for survival on a desert island, from a list of 25 to 30.

HOW TO PLAY

With the class, brainstorm 25 to 30 items found around the house and write them on the board (bottle opener, flashlight, trash bags, twist ties, placemats, bottled water, pet cat, etc.) Any item is okay except those requiring electricity or batteries.

Then, tell the groups to imagine they have just crash-landed on a desert island with no power. Among the items on the board, each group can pick eight they would like to bring for survival. After 15 minutes or so, have the teams report back to the class with their list and why they chose those eight in particular.

WHAT TO LOOK FOR

Students should be negotiating with each other to come up with the final list of items.

Feel free to vary the final number of items. You might also limit the initial list to items found in a particular room, such as the kitchen or bathroom.

Let's Take a Photo

Additional Skills: Speaking, Listening

LEVEL:
3 to 5

GROUP:
4 or 5

10 to 15
MINUTES

MATERIALS & PREP WORK

Prepare photos of groups of people in different poses. For example, you might search Google for "boys [or girls] in different poses."

THE GAME

The object here is for students to work together—purely through words—to reproduce the pose in an existing photograph.

HOW TO PLAY

Divide the students into groups. You'll need the group size to be the number of people in the photo plus one student to act as the photographer. Give the photographer in each group one of the photos.

The photographer cannot show the picture to the others or model any of the poses. He or she is permitted only to use words to get the group to pose like the subject of the photo, and then take an actual photo (assuming that at least one student in the group will have a smartphone). The group that creates a pose closest to the photo wins.

WHAT TO LOOK FOR

The photographer should be communicating with the other students, giving them clear directions on how to pose. Also, make sure that someone in each group has a smartphone— if not, you may need to take the photo yourself.

The more interesting the pose, the more challenging this activity will be for your students, so look for photos with subjects standing and sitting in unexpected positions.

A Night at the Improv

18

LEVEL:
3 to 5

GROUP:
2

🕐

20 to 30
MINUTES

Additional Skills: Speaking, Listening

MATERIALS & PREP WORK

Prepare a set of cards with a pair of role-play characters written on each—for example, customer and café clerk, police officer and bank robber, and waiter and customer.

THE GAME

The object of this activity is for a pair of students to improvise a conversation based on their assumed roles.

HOW TO PLAY

Hand out one role card to each pair and tell the students to choose which person is going to assume which role. Then they need to prepare what each character is going to say. For lower-level students, you might have them write down a dialogue. Higher-level students can be more casual: Suggest they discuss the conversation they would like their characters to have without writing down all the lines. When the students feel ready, call the pairs one by one to the front of the room to present their skits to the class.

WHAT TO LOOK FOR

Lower-level students may need more time to create a dialogue based on their characters.

For a more advanced class, add more detail about the characters. For example, you could have an "angry" customer and an "apologetic" café clerk or a "nervous" police officer and a "dangerous" bank robber.

Video Dialogue

19

Additional Skills: Speaking, Grammar

LEVEL:
3 to 5

GROUP:
3 or 4

10 to 15
MINUTES

MATERIALS & PREP WORK

Prepare a 30- to 60-second video of a scene from a sitcom, like *Seinfeld*, *Big Bang Theory*, *Friends*, or other show of your choice.

THE GAME

The object of the game is for students to create a dialogue based on a soundless video clip.

HOW TO PLAY

Show the video clip several times with the sound off. Then tell the students they need to imagine what the characters in that scene are saying. Their task is to work with their partners to write a script that would make sense with the video they have just watched. Once they have created a script, they need to practice the dialogue. Have them watch the video one more time and, as a final step, say the dialogue aloud along with the video. Once all of the groups have completed this, play the original video clip with the sound to let the students hear what the actual dialogue was.

WHAT TO LOOK FOR

You may want to provide the URL of the video in case the students wish to see it again while they work on their script. Just make sure they don't watch it with the sound.

There is a stop-motion animation series named *Pingu* that I like to use for this activity. Watching this video clip with the sound on may help students imagine the dialogue—but not through actual words. Because the original language of the film is "penguin language," the students have to rely on clues in the characters' intonation to come up with a dialogue. This is something only higher-level students will be able to do.

Wacky Debates

Additional Skills: Speaking, Listening

LEVEL:
3 to 5

GROUP:
2 or 4

20 to 30
MINUTES

MATERIALS & PREP WORK

Prepare cards with debatable topics. These should be weird or at least unusual things—for example, "Frogs should be banned from croaking after nine p.m." or "Restaurants should stop offering free ketchup." A Google search for "old laws still on the books" can provide a great resource for this activity.

THE GAME

The object of the game is for students to debate the topics presented to them on the cards.

HOW TO PLAY

There should be an even number of students in each group. If you have pairs, assign one person to be pro and his or her partner to be con. Give one debate card to each pair. Tell them they have a few minutes to think about their position, and then they can begin debating. If you have groups of four, assign two people to be pro and the other two to be con. Then, give each group one debate card. The "pros" and "cons" can have five minutes to discuss their position in order to prepare for the debate. The pro side can go first and state its opinions, and the debate can begin. Allow the debates to go on for about five minutes. When time is up, the pro students switch to con and the con students switch to pro. Then, give them a new topic card to debate.

WHAT TO LOOK FOR

Lower-level students may need more time to prepare their arguments with their partners.

For more advanced students, you could challenge them further by reducing or eliminating the preparation time.

What's Missing?

21

Additional Skills: Speaking, Listening

LEVEL:
3 to 5

GROUP:
2 or 4

15 to 20
MINUTES

MATERIALS & PREP WORK

Prepare a one- to two-minute clip and script from a TV show involving two speakers. You can usually find the script online; then make two sets of the script. For each set, white out some of the words. For example, in set 1, white out a few words from speaker 1's lines, and in set 2, a few words from speaker 2's lines. Therefore each of these sets will have different words missing. Finally, pick four or five additional words and white them out from both sets, so the two sets have a few identical words missing as well.

THE GAME

The object of the game is to find the missing words in a script from a short scene of a TV show through asking and answering questions.

HOW TO PLAY

Have students sit with their partners and then hand out the scripts. Half of each pair or group gets a script from set 1, and the other half gets a script from set 2. Play the video clip with the sound off once or twice, so the students can get familiar with the context of the script. Tell the students their script is missing some words, and they need to work with their partners to find them. To add some pressure, you can set a time limit. When the groups have finished, they should role-play the dialogue. Then play the clip with the sound on so they can check their work.

WHAT TO LOOK FOR

You'll know it's working when the students have gotten to the stage where they are role-playing the scene. For groups that finish early, help them out with the intonation as they read.

> You can create more than two versions of the altered script and use this activity for a mixer.

22

Wild Conversation Starters

Additional Skills: Speaking, Listening

MATERIALS & PREP WORK

Prepare a set of 10 to 12 cards with bold, attention-grabbing statements—for example, "I'm never going back to that restaurant again," "I can't believe what she said," "My boss is crazy," or "It was the worst party I've ever been to." You will need one set of cards for each pair of students.

THE GAME

The object of the game is for students to create a conversation based on the opening line provided on the card.

HOW TO PLAY

Demonstrate the activity by writing the following prompt on the board: "What happened?" Read a statement aloud from one of the cards, like "I'm never going back to that restaurant again," then elicit a conversation from the class by pointing to the prompt. Once the class gets the idea, have the students sit in pairs, and hand out the cards. One student draws a card and speaks the line. The partner replies with the prompt, "What happened?" and they discuss for two to three minutes. Then another card is drawn, and the partners begin a new conversation.

WHAT TO LOOK FOR

Make sure that the students are asking and answering follow-up questions to develop their conversations.

For higher-level students, give one card to each person and do the activity as a mixer. Put three minutes on the timer, and when time is up, have them exchange cards as well as switch partners.

Listening Games

Time to Go

Additional Skills: Listening, Vocabulary

LEVEL:
1 to 2

GROUP:
4 or 5

🕐
10 to 15 MINUTES

MATERIALS & PREP WORK

Prepare a set of pictures or drawings of at least 20 analog clocks, all set to various times of day. You'll need one set for each group in the class. Also prepare a list of the indicated times.

THE GAME

The object of the game is for students to accurately identify the time on a clock when they hear expressions of time spoken by the teacher.

HOW TO PLAY

It's best if the students can stand around a table. Each team of students gets one set of pictures of analog clocks and lays them on a table faceup. You have a corresponding list of times, such as "10 to five," "a quarter past eight," "half past three," and "five past nine." Read off one time, and the first team to identify which analog clock represents your words gets the point for that round.

WHAT TO LOOK FOR

This is a good activity as a follow-up to a lesson on how to express time in English.

You could turn this into a drawing game. Hand out a worksheet with blank clock faces, and have the groups draw clock hands corresponding to the times you say.

24

Going on a Picnic

Additional Skills: Listening, Speaking

★
LEVEL:
1 to 3

GROUP:
5 or 6

🕐
10
MINUTES

MATERIALS & PREP WORK

Provide a soft foam ball.

THE GAME

This is a memory game where the students say what they are going to bring on a picnic, in addition to repeating the items listed by the previous students.

HOW TO PLAY

Write this sentence on the board: "I'm going on a picnic, and I'm going to bring _____." Throw the ball to a student, who finishes the sentence. "I'm going on a picnic, and I'm going to bring apples." The student then throws the ball to someone else, who repeats the previous sentence and adds what he or she will bring: "I'm going on a picnic, and I'm going to bring apples and bananas." That student throws the ball to someone else, who repeats and continues: "I'm going on a picnic and I'm going to bring apples, bananas, and carrots." This activity continues until a student can't remember all of the items.

WHAT TO LOOK FOR

If you have a large class, you'll need to have several groups doing this activity at the same time, so go around the room helping each group get going.

For lower-level students, restrict the items brought to food. More advanced students can play without restrictions.

Crazy Rhymes

25

Additional Skills: Listening, Vocabulary, Spelling

★
LEVEL:
1 to 3

👤
GROUP:
3 or 4

🕐
10 to 15
MINUTES

MATERIALS & PREP WORK

Prepare a list of simple words that can be easily rhymed.

THE GAME

The object of the game is for students to come up with a list of words that rhyme with the given target word provided by the teacher. Since this focuses on rhyming, it reinforces listening skills.

HOW TO PLAY

Rhyming could be a new concept for some of your students, depending on their native language or country. Because of this, it's a good idea to demonstrate what a rhyme is. Write a word on the board, like *bed*. Then, write a few words that rhyme with *bed*, like *bread*, *red*, and *head*. Point out to the students that even though the spelling is different, the sound of the words is the same.

Once you feel everyone in the class is on board, begin the game. Tell the groups that you will give them a word, then they will work together to write a list of words that rhyme with the one you provided them. Write another word on the board (or say it), and give the groups a time limit of one to two minutes to formulate their lists.

WHAT TO LOOK FOR

Make sure the students are working as a group and not just silently writing words. They need to discover and practice the words with the rhyming sound.

For higher-level students, you could require the word list to match both the rhyme of the target word and the syllable count as well. Also, keep in mind that lower-level students may need help with spelling.

26

Listening Cloze

Additional Skills: Listening, Writing

★

LEVEL:
1 to 3

GROUP:
2 or 3

10 to 15
MINUTES

MATERIALS & PREP WORK

Prepare a worksheet with a dialogue from the textbook, and white out some of the key vocabulary, verbs, prepositions, and so on, depending on the language point being studied. You will also need a recording of the dialogue for this activity.

THE GAME

The object of the game is to guess which words are missing from a dialogue.

HOW TO PLAY

Hand out a copy of the worksheet to each student. Tell the class the worksheet presents a conversation but that it contains some blank spaces. Ask the students to work in groups to guess what those missing words might be. Once they are done, shuffle the students into new groups and ask them to check their answers with their new partners. Then, play the recording so they can listen to the complete version and check their guesses.

WHAT TO LOOK FOR

Students should be communicating with each other, asking questions like "What do you think should go in the blank?"

For more advanced classes, you can focus on erasing particular grammatical elements, like prepositions or articles such as *a* and *the*.

What Am I Doing?

Additional Skills: Listening, Speaking, Grammar (present continuous)

LEVEL:
2 to 5

GROUP:
4 or 5

15 to 20 MINUTES

MATERIALS & PREP WORK

Prepare a set of cards with various activities (shaving, cooking, studying, swimming, etc.) written on them. You will need one set of cards for each group of students.

THE GAME

The object of the game is for students to guess the activity their partner is describing by listening to clues and asking questions.

HOW TO PLAY

Write the key sentence on the board, "You are _____," and tell the students they need to guess what you are doing. For a card that says "boiling eggs," give the students a clue—for example, "I do this with water." With this clue in mind, another student tries to guess using the key sentence format, suggesting, "You are making tea." You say, "Good guess, but no." Continue to give clues until a student correctly guesses the activity, then hand out a set of cards to each group. Remember that the student who draws the first card can give only one clue at a time, and there can be only one guess following each clue. The student in each group to correctly guess the activity goes next.

WHAT TO LOOK FOR

Make sure all students in the group are participating and that they follow the one-clue/one-guess rule.

For higher-level students, try using more creative activities, such as "flying my spaceship" or "sailing in my submarine."

Find the Mistake Dictation

28

★
LEVEL:
2 to 5

GROUP:
3 or 4

🕐
10 to 15
MINUTES

Additional Skills: Listening, Grammar

MATERIALS & PREP WORK

Prepare sentences, both correct and incorrect, based on a grammar point you have been working on recently or one you would like to review.

THE GAME

This game is meant to help students practice their listening skills while learning to identify grammatical errors. Having listened to the teacher read two sentences—one correct and another incorrect—students write both down and determine which is which.

HOW TO PLAY

Tell the students that you're going to read some sentences that they will write down. To demonstrate, read one correct sentence a single time.

Ask the students to work with their groups to make sure they take down the sentence correctly. The idea is that with three or four students working together, they should be able to come up with the sentence as a group. When the students are ready, the activity can begin. Tell the class that you are now going to read a set of two sentences, which they need to write down exactly as spoken. Now explain that one of the sentences in the set contains a mistake. After they have written down the sentences, the students must work with their groups to identify which sentence is the one with the error.

WHAT TO LOOK FOR

Look around the room to make sure the students are working in groups to complete this activity. They should be able to ask their classmates questions about what they heard.

You can turn this into a review activity by using grammar or vocabulary patterns that you studied during the past few classes.

29

Police Sketch

Additional Skills: Listening, Speaking
(descriptive adjectives)

LEVEL:
2 to 5

GROUP:
4

10 to 15
MINUTES

MATERIALS & PREP WORK

Prepare some photos of different faces. Try to find photos of people with distinguishing features, such as a moustache, a beard, or eyeglasses.

THE GAME

The object of the game is for one student to describe an image of a person's face in detail and then for classmates to try to draw a picture of that face.

HOW TO PLAY

Give one student in each group a picture and tell him or her not to show the picture to the rest of the group. This student is called the describer. The describer has to describe the face in the picture to the group. Then the other students have to listen to the description and draw the face as their classmate speaks, like the police sketch of a criminal based on the witness's description. When they are finished, they show their drawings to the describer, who then decides which is the best one. The artist of that drawing gets a point. Then, the person sitting to the right of the describer takes a turn as the describer, and play continues. The game is over when all four students have had a chance to describe a picture. The student with the most points is declared the winner.

WHAT TO LOOK FOR

Make sure that the student describing a picture is giving as much detail as possible.

For lower-level students, you may want to help them by first eliciting and then writing a list of key vocabulary on the board.

Who Said That?

30

Additional Skills: Listening, Vocabulary, Spelling

LEVEL:
2 to 5

GROUP:
4 or 5

**10
MINUTES**

MATERIALS & PREP WORK

Prepare a set of cards with statements that someone with a particular job would say—for example, "Please show me your driver's license and insurance card," "Would you like fries with that?" and "Stick out your tongue and say, 'Ahhh.'" You will need one set for each group.

THE GAME

The object of the game is to match common statements with the occupations of those who say them.

HOW TO PLAY

Demonstrate this activity by brainstorming occupations on the board. Then, using the list you've just created, make a statement that someone with one of those occupations would say. For example, the word *carpenter* is on the board. You say, "Please pass the hammer." Elicit from the class who would say that. Once the students get the idea, have them sit in their groups, and give each group a set of cards. Taking turns, each student draws a card and reads it aloud. The first student in the group to identify who would say the line written on it wins the card. The student with the most cards at the end is the winner.

WHAT TO LOOK FOR

You'll know it's working when you see the students smoothly guessing the occupations. You can allow the group to skip a card if nobody can guess it.

Higher-level students may not need the brainstorming activity at the beginning.

31

How's the Weather?

Additional Skills: Listening (weather-related vocabulary)

LEVEL:
3 to 5

GROUP:
2

10 to 15 MINUTES

MATERIALS & PREP WORK

Prepare a sound file of a weather report from YouTube or the radio. A local forecast is always better and more relevant to the students.

THE GAME

The object of the game is for students to listen to a weather broadcast and then write down all of the weather-related words they hear (*clear, rainy, hot, chilly,* etc.). You could also include numbers regarding temperature, wind speed, and so on.

HOW TO PLAY

If needed, look to your class for weather-related vocabulary (as mentioned above) and write it on the board. Then, ask the pairs to write today's weather report for your city. This will get them thinking about the different parts of the weather report—for example, temperature, sky condition, precipitation, and wind. After reviewing this with the whole class, tell the students you are going to play a recording of a weather report. Their task is to write down all of the weather-related vocabulary words they hear. This listening activity can be further broken down into parts of the day—for example, this morning, this afternoon, tonight, and tomorrow, depending on your weather report clip and the class level.

WHAT TO LOOK FOR

The key phrases for this activity are "What did you hear?" and "I heard . . ." Make sure the students are working cooperatively and communicating with each other about what they heard.

For lower-level classes, you can prepare a transcript of the weather report and make it a cloze listening activity.

32

Card on the Head

Additional Skills: Listening, Speaking, Vocabulary

LEVEL:
3 to 5

GROUP:
4 or 5

🕐
15 to 20
MINUTES

MATERIALS & PREP WORK

Prepare cards with whatever vocabulary you'd like to practice. This game can be played with nouns, verbs, and adjectives alike.

THE GAME

The object of the game is for the student holding the card against his or her forehead to guess the word written on it by listening to the clues given by classmates.

HOW TO PLAY

In front of the class, tell the students that you are going to show them a word without looking at it yourself. They have to try and make you say that word by giving you clues, but they cannot say the word. I like to use *milk* as a demonstration word because it's easy to give clues: "It's white." "It's a drink." "It comes from a cow."

Have students sit in groups of four or five in a circle. Hand out a set of cards to each group, and place the cards face-down in the center. The students should take turns drawing a card and placing it on their forehead, where they cannot read it themselves but the others in their group can. The other students then need to give clues to the one with the card to make him or her guess the word.

WHAT TO LOOK FOR

You'll know it's working when all of the members in each group are actively participating and giving clues.

For lower-level students, you might allow them to gesture or mime if they don't have enough vocabulary to give successful clues.

33

Private Party

Additional Skills: Listening, Vocabulary

★
LEVEL:
3 to 5

GROUP:
WHOLE
CLASS

🕐
10 to 15
MINUTES

MATERIALS & PREP WORK

None.

THE GAME

In this game, students must work out the teacher's secret code by listening carefully to the questions and answers of the other students.

HOW TO PLAY

Tell the students, "I'm having a private party. If you bring the right thing, you can come to the party." However, you have a secret code—students can come only if their answer follows the code. This code might be words beginning with a vowel, words with a single syllable, or words within a particular category, such as fruit or drinks.

Let's imagine you decide the code is single-syllable words. One student says, "I'm going to bring cheese." You answer, "You can come to the party." A second student says, "I'm going to bring wine." You respond, "You can come to the party, too." Then a third student says, "I'm going to bring music." To this, you respond, "Sorry, you can't come." Play continues until all students have broken the code and can come to the party.

WHAT TO LOOK FOR

You can ask students to write down the words their class-mates say, as this can sometimes help give them visual clues about the code.

Instead of playing this game with the whole group, you can have the students work in pairs. Having a partner may be easier for lower-level students.

Truth or Lie

34

Additional Skills: Listening, Speaking

LEVEL:
3 to 5

GROUP:
4 or 5

15 to 20
MINUTES

MATERIALS & PREP WORK

Prepare cards with several topics similar to the essay-writing topics of the TOEFL exam—for example, "Which do you prefer, living in the city or the countryside?" and "They propose to build a movie theater in your town. Do you support or oppose it?" You will need one set for each group of students.

THE GAME

The object of the game is for students to decide if their partner is telling the truth or a lie.

HOW TO PLAY

To demonstrate, draw a card, read it, and offer your opinion on the card's topic. Then ask the students if they think that you gave your true opinion or told a lie. Tell the students that they are going to repeat the same process in their groups, so they really need to put on their best poker face. Distribute a set of cards to each group and begin. One student in the group picks a card, reads it, and gives an opinion. The other team members then need to determine if that student is giving a true opinion or a false one.

WHAT TO LOOK FOR

Make sure the student who is stating an opinion is giving a few reasons for that opinion.

In addition to the cards with the topics, you can force students to give an opinion that is either the truth or a lie by passing out cards that say "truth" or "lie." Then, the student giving an opinion has to do so based on whether he or she has a truth card or a lie card. For example, a student draws the card "Which do you prefer, living in the city or the countryside?" In addition, the student draws a lie card. If this person prefers living in the city, he or she must pretend to prefer living in the countryside, which is a lie.

35

What Did You Catch?

Additional Skills: Listening, Speaking, Questions

LEVEL:
3 to 5

GROUP:
3 or 4

10 MINUTES

MATERIALS & PREP WORK

Prepare a short clip (two to three minutes) of a scene from a sitcom, like *Seinfeld, Big Bang Theory,* or *Friends*, or a news report.

THE GAME

In this game, students engage in a collective listening activity. The goal is to exchange information by asking and answering questions about the scene.

HOW TO PLAY

Many English textbooks have a listening task followed by comprehension questions. In this activity, the students write their own comprehension questions based on an audio they listen to or a video they watch. Have the students sit with their partners and play the clip a couple of times. If it is a video, you could also provide them with the link, so they can watch it on their smartphones. Put six or seven minutes on a timer, and tell the groups they need to come up with at least three questions about the clip. When they are finished, have them ask and answer each other's questions.

WHAT TO LOOK FOR

Students should be writing questions about who, what, when, where, and so on.

For lower-level students, you might substitute the video clip for a dialogue or other audio from your class textbook.

Writing &
Reading
Games

What's the Question?

36

Additional Skills: Writing (questions), Grammar

LEVEL:
1 to 4

GROUP:
3

🕑
20 to 25
MINUTES

MATERIALS & PREP WORK

Prepare a handout with a list of 20 different kinds of nouns, including names, places, people, and dates—for example, Mozart, the Amazon River, banana, March 10th, and so on.

THE GAME

The object of the game is to come up with the longest list of questions that could be answered by the words on the handout.

HOW TO PLAY

Give a copy of the handout to each student, and then have the students sit with their partners. Demonstrate the activity by writing a word on the board—for example, *Mozart*. Then, ask for questions whose answer could be "Mozart," such as, "What is the name a famous composer starting with *M*?" "Which composer wrote *The Magic Flute*?" and "What was Wolfgang Amadeus's last name?" Put 20 minutes on the timer, and tell the students they need to come up with as many questions as possible about each word on the handout. The group with the most questions at the end of the time allowed wins.

WHAT TO LOOK FOR

The students should be working together to come up with a single list of questions.

You can vary the list of terms on the handout based on your location and the cultural backgrounds of the students.

Picture Story

Additional Skills: Writing, Grammar, Vocabulary

LEVEL:
2 to 5

GROUP:
2 or 3

15 to 20
MINUTES

MATERIALS & PREP WORK

Prepare a strange or unusual photo. For example, search Google Images for "Minnie Mouse is cheating on Mickey Mouse with Goofy" or "funny Christmas fails compilation."

THE GAME

The object of the game is for students to come up with an original story based on a strange or unusual photo.

HOW TO PLAY

You can demonstrate this activity by showing the class one of the strange photos you found. Ask the class questions, such as "Who is in the photo?" "Where are they?" "What are they doing in the photo?" and "What do you think they were they doing before the photo was taken?" Then tell the students you are going to give them their own photos to study. Give each pair or group a copy of another photo, and tell them they have 15 minutes to write a story explaining the situation. At the end of this period, the groups present their stories to the class.

WHAT TO LOOK FOR

Even though the students work in pairs or small groups, each student should be writing the story (and it should be the same story), so they should be communicating with one another.

For lower-level classes, you may want to write the questions on the board to help them generate ideas for their stories.

Two Truths, One Fib

Additional Skills: Writing, Listening, Speaking

LEVEL:
2 to 5

GROUP:
2 to 4

10 to 15
MINUTES

MATERIALS & PREP WORK

None.

THE GAME

The object of the game is for students to guess which one of three statements made by their partner is a fib.

HOW TO PLAY

Demonstrate this activity by writing three sentences on the board about what you did last weekend. Make sure that one of them is not true but also that it would be hard to guess whether the other two were true or not. For example, you could tell the students, "I played tennis" as well as

"I cooked breakfast for my family" and "I walked the dog after breakfast." Then tell them one of those statements is not true. Put three minutes on the timer, and tell them they need to discuss the statements with their partners to decide which statement is a fib. Once they get the idea, they can write their own three sentences, show them to the group, and see if they can fool their partners.

WHAT TO LOOK FOR

Make sure the students are discussing the statements with their partners to come up with a consensus as to which one is untrue.

> You can vary the topic—for example, focus on "what I did last night," "my hometown," or "my family."

Jungle Diaries

39

Additional Skills: Writing, Listening, Speaking

LEVEL:
3 to 5

GROUP:
2 or 3

15 to 20 MINUTES

MATERIALS & PREP WORK

None.

THE GAME

The object of this game is to get the students to work together to write a diary entry from the point of view of a wild animal, insect, or pet.

HOW TO PLAY

To get the students thinking in the right frame of mind, ask them some questions about their day. For example, ask, "What time did you wake up?" "How was the weather then?" "How did you feel at that time and why?" or "What did you do after you woke up?" Then tell the students that each group needs to choose a specific animal. It could be any type of wild creature, an insect, or even a pet. Their job is to write a diary entry from that animal's point of view, with as much detail as they can imagine.

WHAT TO LOOK FOR

Ensure that the students are working together and discussing how the story unfolds, even though they should all be writing down the story.

You can vary this activity to make the animal a cartoon or animation figure, such as one of the Disney animal characters or Hello Kitty.

Rappin' ABCs

40

Additional Skills: Writing, Vocabulary, Speaking (intonation)

LEVEL:
3 to 5

GROUP:
3 or 4

20 to 30 MINUTES

MATERIALS & PREP WORK

Find some rap background music tracks on YouTube, or have your students search for them on their smartphones.

THE GAME

In this game, students create a simple rap lyric using both rhyme and alphabetical order.

HOW TO PLAY

Tell the students they are going to come up with the next big rap music hit using their own original lyrics. Write the following model on the board: "A spells Apple and B makes Boy, S starts Super and T gives us Toy." Then tell them to create a lyric like this by following these rules:

1. Start with a letter, a verb or phrase, and a word starting with that letter ("*A* spells *apple*").
2. The two words in each line must begin with consecutive letters in the alphabet (*A* and *B*, then *S* and *T*).
3. End the first and second lines with key words that rhyme (*boy* and *toy*).

WHAT TO LOOK FOR

If you give the students the okay to choose their own backing track, make sure they don't spend more time researching this than writing the lyric.

If rap is not your thing, you can turn this into a poetry or nursery rhyme activity. The students still write the "lyric," just without the backbeat.

Seuss Tales

LEVEL:
3 to 5

GROUP:
3 or 4

15 to 20
MINUTES

Additional Skills: Writing, Spelling,
Pronunciation, Vocabulary

MATERIALS & PREP WORK

Prepare a page or two from the Dr. Seuss book
A Wocket in My Pocket.

THE GAME

The object of the game is for the students to
demonstrate their knowledge of vocabulary,
phonics, and pronunciation by writing a
Seuss-like verse.

HOW TO PLAY

This is a creative writing activity based loosely on
the Dr. Seuss book that features verse like "…a
WASKET in your BASKET? Or a NUREAU in your
BUREAU? Or a WOSET in your CLOSET?" Students
work in groups, and each group is assigned a

different room in the house (bathroom, bedroom, kitchen, garage, etc.). They need to first come up with a list of 10 or 15 items in that room. For example, the kitchen will include a sink, dishwasher, toaster, and so on. Then, they Seuss it up with simple sentences and nonsense rhymes, such as "I saw a dink in my sink, a boaster in my toaster, and a mishmasher in the dishwasher."

WHAT TO LOOK FOR

Lower-level students may have trouble coming up with rhyming words. You can tell them one easy trick is to simply change the first few letters to make a new word (e.g., *dink* instead of *sink*).

For higher-level students, you might ask them to come up with verses containing more alliteration patterns, for example, "I saw a susink in my sink, a toliboaster in my toaster and a dillymasher in the dishwasher."

Stray Cat Strut

Additional Skills: Writing, Grammar, Vocabulary

LEVEL:
3 to 5

GROUP:
2

30 MINUTES

MATERIALS & PREP WORK

None.

THE GAME

The object of the game is for students to write a story from the perspective of a stray neighborhood cat that someone has brought home and kept as a pet.

HOW TO PLAY

Tell the students they are going to write a story with their partner. Here is the premise: A stray cat had been living in the neighborhood for a long time. One day, someone found the cat and

ESL GAMES FOR THE CLASSROOM

decided to give it a home. Assuming the perspective of the cat, write a page or two about what happened next. Some questions to prompt the writing include "Who found you?" "What are they like?" "Where do they live?" "What is your new family like (if more than one person)"? and "How is your life now compared to when you were a stray?"

WHAT TO LOOK FOR

Lower-level students in particular may need prompts, such as the questions above, to give them ideas for writing the story.

For higher-level classes, feel free to adjust the story and substitute a different animal, such as a dog or rabbit, or even a wild animal, like a monkey.

Weekday Update!

Additional Skills: Writing, Speaking

★
LEVEL:
3 to 5

GROUP:
2

🕐
40 to 60
MINUTES

MATERIALS & PREP WORK

Prepare a handout with a list of interesting or weird news headlines, such as those from the *National Enquirer* or the *Star*—for example, "Man Discovers Alien in His Bathtub," "Elvis Found Living in Jungle," "Half Man, Half Bird Found at the Grand Canyon," and so on. If you have one of those newspapers, you could provide the students with the headline and the accompanying photo.

THE GAME

The object of the game is for students to create and present a news story based on a headline and picture they receive.

HOW TO PLAY

Give a copy of the handout to each student. Tell them each pair will have 15 minutes to write a news story based on one of the headlines on the handout, using the following format common in TV news broadcasts: The announcer introduces the story with some basic information, followed by a reporter on the scene giving the details. Each pair of students should work together to write both these parts of the news report. When they have finished, they should come to the front of the room to sit at the "news desk" and report their story to the class.

WHAT TO LOOK FOR

Make sure the students include as much detail as possible, including who, when, where, what, why, and how.

> For this activity, you can give either a different news story to each pair or the same news story to all pairs.

Weird Dreams

44

Additional Skills: Writing, Speaking

LEVEL:
3 to 5

GROUP:
2 or 3

🕐
20 to 30
MINUTES

MATERIALS & PREP WORK

None.

THE GAME

The object of the game is for students to create the story of a dream they had the night before.

HOW TO PLAY

Write the following on the board: "I had a weird dream last night. I was at the beach, and a fish started walking out of the sea." Tell the students that this is the beginning of a story describing a dream. They will have about 15 minutes to work with their partners to complete the rest of the story—that is, what happened next and how the dream ends. With their partner or group, the students need to come up with the story, and each person should write it down.

WHAT TO LOOK FOR

Make sure that the students are working together to compose the story and not just writing silently.

For variety, you could prepare a handout with several dream-starting sentences and then assign a particular dream to each group of students.

Broken Conversation

45

★
LEVEL:
1 to 4

GROUP:
2 or 3

10 to 15
MINUTES

Additional Skills: Reading, Listening,
Speaking (asking for/giving opinions)

MATERIALS & PREP WORK

Prepare a dialogue from the class textbook, an
excerpt from a TV program, or an original dialogue.
Make enough copies so there is one for each pair
or group. Then, cut each copy into strips of one
line of dialogue each.

THE GAME

The object of this game is to successfully place
strips of dialogue into their original order. The
students need to work as a team to complete
this activity.

HOW TO PLAY

Give one set of dialogue strips to each pair or group. First the students need to read each strip, so tell them to take turns reading. Then, they have to work together to reassemble the strips into a logical conversation. You can either give them a time limit or make the activity a competition simply by stating that the first team to complete the task is the winner. At the end of the activity, play a recording of the dialogue so the students can check their work.

WHAT TO LOOK FOR

Make sure the students are communicating with each other and not just working in silence.

Have higher-level students work in pairs, and at the end of the activity, ask the pairs to role-play the dialogue. The rest of the class can vote on which pair read the dialogue with the best pronunciation, intonation, and expression.

46

It's the Law

Additional Skills: Reading, Speaking, Listening

LEVEL:
2 to 5

GROUP:
3 or 4

⏱
15 to 20
MINUTES

MATERIALS & PREP WORK

Make a list of 15 to 20 weird laws still on the books in the United States. You can find a number of these laws by searching online for "weird laws in America." Prepare a handout with the laws but with one key word (a noun) missing from each—for example, "In New York, it is illegal to wear _____ after 10 p.m."; "In Hawaii, you are not allowed to put _____ in someone's ear"; and "In Nevada, it is illegal to drive a _____ on the highway." Include a list of the missing words (in random order) on the top of the handout.

THE GAME

The object of the game is for students to guess the missing words in a sentence. The sentence is a weird and outdated law that is still on the books somewhere in the United States.

HOW TO PLAY

Give a handout to each group, and tell the students they need to decide as a group what the missing word is. They must explain to their partners why they chose a particular word, and then everyone in the group must all agree before proceeding. At the end of the activity, you can award points for correct answers.

WHAT TO LOOK FOR

You'll know it's working when the students are discussing why they came up with a particular word or phrase.

> For higher levels, you can prepare the worksheet without including the list of words as potential answers. This encourages the students to use their imagination.

Why Did You Say That?

47

GROUP:
WHOLE
CLASS

10 to 15
MINUTES

Additional Skills: Reading, Listening

MATERIALS & PREP WORK

Prepare a handout with a list of 20 phrases that a person would say in response to something else—for example, "Wow! That's very kind of you"; "Thanks, but I couldn't eat another bite"; "Oh please, go ahead"; and "It was amazing!" Then, prepare a page for yourself with a list of matching first sentences that inspired these responses. For example, "Would you like some more pasta?" is a match for "Thanks, but I couldn't eat another bite."

THE GAME

The object of the game is for students to correctly identify which statement would be an appropriate response to the one spoken by the teacher.

HOW TO PLAY

Demonstrate this activity by writing three responses on the board: "Nice to meet you, John"; "My name is John"; and "This is John." Tell the students you are going to offer a short statement, and they need to decide which of the three responses on the board is the best. Your statement is "Hi, I'm John." Following this setup, distribute the handout to the students. Give them a few minutes to read the phrases written on it, and then start saying your list of sentences.

WHAT TO LOOK FOR

You'll know it's working when the students respond quickly to the sentences you say. Depending on how you wrote the handout, there may be multiple correct matches.

You may want to put the students in pairs or groups of three, so they can collectively work on finding the correct answers.

48

Mixed-Up Stories

Additional Skills: Reading, Listening, Speaking

LEVEL:
3 to 5

GROUP:
3 or 4

10 to 15
MINUTES

MATERIALS & PREP WORK

Prepare three or four short stories, like "Little Red Riding Hood," "The Three Little Pigs," and "Jack and the Beanstalk." Cut each story into strips of one sentence each. Take one strip from each story and exchange it for one strip in another story. This means that each set of story strips will contain one sentence that doesn't belong—this swap is what makes this activity challenging.

THE GAME

The object of the game is for students to place a bunch of jumbled sentences back into their correct order: the story they originally were.

HOW TO PLAY

Give each group one story cut into strips. Each person in the group should read one or two of the strips, then place them on the table in front of the group. Then, the group needs to work together to figure out the correct order of the sentence strips. In addition to this, the students need to figure out which of the sentences does not belong to their story. At this point they need to connect with another group of students to exchange their "extra sentences" so that each group ends up with a complete story.

WHAT TO LOOK FOR

You may need to assist students with vocabulary questions, depending on the story you have chosen.

For lower-level students, you may prefer not to mix sentences from other stories. Instead, focus the students' efforts on placing the sentences in the correct order.

Vocabulary
Games

Opposite Concentration

49

LEVEL:
1 to 3

GROUP:
3

10 to 15
MINUTES

Additional Skills: Vocabulary

MATERIALS AND PREP WORK

Prepare a set of cards with adjectives and their opposites (like *hot, cold, big, small*) and other words with opposite meanings (like *up, down, yes, no*), with one word on each card. There should be 36 cards per set, and you should have enough sets for the number of groups in your class.

THE GAME

The object of the game is for students to match words with their opposites.

HOW TO PLAY

Give one set of cards to each group, and have the groups place the cards in front of them facedown in a gridlike pattern of six cards by six cards. The first student turns over two cards and reads the words on the cards. If those two words don't have opposite meanings, the cards can remain faceup, and that student can go again. Play continues for that student until he or she has uncovered two cards that do have opposite meanings. When that happens, the student must turn the unmatched cards facedown once again, and the next student in the group gets to go. The game is over when all cards have been left faceup.

WHAT TO LOOK FOR

Make sure that the students are reading the cards aloud as they turn them over and not just working silently.

To add an extra challenge to this game, tell the students that once they have a match, they need to make one sentence using both words—for example, "Ice cream is cold, but cocoa is hot."

Picture-ary

50

Additional Skills: Vocabulary, Spelling

LEVEL:
1 to 3

GROUP:
DIVIDE
THE CLASS
INTO TWO
TEAMS

🕐
10 to 15
MINUTES

MATERIALS & PREP WORK

Prepare cards that each have a topic and corresponding clues written on them. For example, card 1 could read "TOPIC: Things starting with the letter *F*. CLUES: Football, face, fork." Card 2 could read, "TOPIC: Things you can drink. CLUES: Coffee, beer, wine." Card 3 could read, "TOPIC: Things you do in the kitchen. CLUES: Cook, eat, wash dishes."

THE GAME

The object of the game is for the students to guess a vocabulary word based on a picture drawn by their teammates.

HOW TO PLAY

Demonstrate the game at the whiteboard by taking a card and telling the students the topic: "The topic is things starting with the letter *F*."

Then draw an image of a face to elicit the word *face* from the students. Once they get the idea, you can begin the game. Divide the class into two groups. Have each group choose one student to draw first, and then decide which group will be the first to go. Hand the student a card and tell him or her to announce the topic, choose a word from the category, and draw a picture of it on the whiteboard. If that person's team guesses the word, the team wins the point, and the next person on the team can draw the next picture. If the other team guesses the word first, then that team gets the point and goes on to draw the next picture instead.

WHAT TO LOOK FOR

Encourage all the students to participate and try to guess the word.

If you have a very large class, you may prefer to have two games going at the same time, as long as you have two whiteboards.

51

Languages and Countries

Additional Skills: Vocabulary, Spelling, Listening

LEVEL:
1 to 3

GROUP:
3 or 4

10 to 15 MINUTES

MATERIALS & PREP WORK

Prepare a list of countries and their corresponding languages, like *Spain/Spanish*, *Russia/Russian*, and so on.

THE GAME

The object of the game is to practice the vocabulary of countries (nouns) and their related languages (adjectives).

HOW TO PLAY

First model the activity. Ask the students where they are right now, and write the name of that country on the board. Then ask the students what language is spoken in that country, and write that on the board as well. Tell the students you are going to say either the name of a country or its language, and they'll need to work with their partners to come up with either the name of the language spoken in the given country or the name of the country in which one speaks the given language. When they are ready to answer, they must also be able to spell their answers. The first group that can answer correctly wins the point.

WHAT TO LOOK FOR

The students should be working together to agree upon the answers for the group.

Keep in mind there are some irregularities. For example, Portuguese is spoken in both Brazil and Portugal, and Holland is an older name for the Netherlands, where they speak Dutch.

52

Question Word Match

LEVEL:
1 to 3

GROUP: WHOLE CLASS

10 to 15 MINUTES

Additional Skills: Vocabulary (question words), Spelling

MATERIALS & PREP WORK

Prepare two sets of cards with random questions using question words, such as *what, how, when,* and so on. Write the initial question words on one set of cards and the remainder of the questions on the other set. For example, write "What" on one card and "color is a lemon?" on another card; "How" on one card and "many students are in this class?" on another card; and "When" on one card and "was the Internet invented?" on another card. Make enough so that each student will have two cards from either one set or the other.

THE GAME

In this game, each student receives a card with part of a question written on it. The object is to find the person whose card completes the question.

HOW TO PLAY

Divide the class in half. Give half the students two cards each from the question-word set, and give the other half two cards each from the other set. Then, have a mixer. The students need to go around the classroom to find the students who can provide the matches to both of their cards. The first group of students to come up with a complete set of questions wins the game.

WHAT TO LOOK FOR

To find a match, students should be asking each other questions, not just showing each other their cards.

For higher-level students, you might ask them to write the answers to the questions once they've found the correct match.

53

That's Not Regular: Singular or Plural?

LEVEL:
1 to 3

GROUP:
2 or 3

10
MINUTES

Additional Skills: Vocabulary

MATERIALS & PREP WORK

Prepare a handout with depictions of the following singular and plural nouns, as shown in the illustration: cactus/cacti, child/children, fish/fish, foot/feet, goose/geese, man/men, mouse/mice, person/people, shrimp/shrimp, tooth/teeth, trout/trout, woman/women. You will need one copy for each student.

THE GAME

The object of the game is to properly identify and write the singular and plural forms of irregular nouns illustrated in the handout.

HOW TO PLAY

Hand out a copy of the illustrated worksheet to each student and have the students sit in pairs or groups of three. To demonstrate the activity, draw a stick figure on the board, and then below it, draw a group of stick figures. Write the letter *p* next to each drawing. Elicit the words *person* and *people* from the class. Tell the students they need to work with their partners to similarly write the singular and plural forms of the nouns based on the illustrations in the handout. The first team finished is the winner.

WHAT TO LOOK FOR

Lower-level students may need a list of the nouns on the handout to help them with the activity.

Download a free worksheet for this game at callistomediabooks.com/esl-games.

Strange Stories

54

Additional Skills: Vocabulary (parts of speech), Spelling

LEVEL:
1 to 3

GROUP:
3 or 4

10 to 15
MINUTES

MATERIALS & PREP WORK

Prepare two handouts. Page 1 is a story, like a fairy tale, with various words (nouns, verbs, adverbs, adjectives, time words, etc.) whited out. Each of these spaces should have a number. On the second page, make a list of numbers with a blank space and what kind of word should be written there (noun, verb, adverb, adjective, time word, etc.), corresponding to the numbered spaces on page 1.

THE GAME

This game allows students to practice the different parts of speech in an entertaining cloze story exercise.

HOW TO PLAY

Hand out page 2 to each student. They are to fill in each blank space with an appropriate word (noun, verb, adverb, adjective, time word, etc.) individually. When they are done, give each group one copy of the story. The students then take turns reading the story, inserting words from their own list as they read. When all the students have read the story, the members of the group can vote for which is the best or funniest story in the group.

WHAT TO LOOK FOR

Encourage the students to use a wide variety of vocabulary, especially adjectives and adverbs.

For lower-level students, your handout (page 2) could include your own list of nouns, verbs, adverbs, adjectives, time words, and so on for the students to choose from.

Phonics Drill

55

Additional Skills: Vocabulary, Spelling

LEVEL:
1 to 4

GROUP:
3 or 4

10 to 15
MINUTES

MATERIALS & PREP WORK

Prepare a list of words with different phonetic combinations, for example, *cat*, *put*, and *apple*.

THE GAME

The object of the game is for students to come up with a list of words that have the same phonics sound as the teacher's example.

HOW TO PLAY

Write a word on the board, such as *cat*. Then, circle the phonetic combination *at*. Tell the groups that they have only one minute to come up with a list of words that contain the same sound, for example, *bat*, *attic*, and *that*. The group with the longest list after one minute wins the point. Then continue with the next word.

WHAT TO LOOK FOR

Make sure the students speak aloud the words they call to mind and don't just work in silence.

If you like, you can make this into a rhyming activity. This means that the students must come up with a list of words that rhyme with the phonics sound at the end of the primary word.

Best Match

56

Additional Skills: Vocabulary (collocations), Listening

★
LEVEL:
1 to 5

GROUP:
3 or 4

🕐
10 to 15
MINUTES

MATERIALS & PREP WORK

Prepare a list of nouns. It can be a set of similar nouns (like a list of fruit or animals) or a collection of random nouns (*apple*, *desk*, *mountain*).

THE GAME

This is a vocabulary matching game with adjectives and nouns. The object of the game is to come up with adjectives that collocate or appear often with a particular noun.

HOW TO PLAY

Call out the first noun or write it on the board. The groups of students work together to come up with a list of adjectives that can be logically placed with that particular noun. The collocation has to make sense. For example, if the noun is *cat*, then *black*, *cute*, *hungry*, and so on would be acceptable, but *square*, *hard*, or *hard-working* would not be okay here. The team with the most adjectives for that noun wins the point. For added pressure and more excitement, give the groups a time limit.

WHAT TO LOOK FOR

Make sure the students work as a team to come up with the list of collocations. They need to write out the adjective-noun pairings (e.g., "black cat") and not just the adjectives themselves.

For each group and for each round, have the students take turns being the scribe. For fun, you can also decide if you want to accept funny or weird collocations, like "delicious cat" or "dangerous banana."

57

Password

Additional Skills: Vocabulary, Listening

LEVEL:
1 to 5

GROUP:
2

15 to 20
MINUTES

MATERIALS & PREP WORK

Choose a category, such as animals, fruit, or sports.
Prepare a set of cards with one example of the
category written on each card. You may also want
to label the category at the top of the cards. You
will need one set of cards for each pair of students.

THE GAME

The object of the game is for students to guess the
vocabulary word written on their partner's card.

HOW TO PLAY

Like the old TV quiz game, this offers a good
vocabulary review. Have students sit in pairs
and demonstrate how the game works. Tell the

students that fruit is the category, and write the word *fruit* on the board. Explain that they need to guess which type of fruit you have in mind. You can offer only one-word clues, and they must guess with single words in response. For example, if the word is *apple*, your clues might include "pie," "red," and "juice." From these hints, the class guesses the word. Then hand out a set of cards to each pair, and let them play the game.

WHAT TO LOOK FOR

The challenging part of this activity is that the speaker and guesser can use only one word at a time.

If you have access to a computer and a projector, you can find an old clip of the original *Password* TV show to show your students before playing the game.

58

Crazy Descriptions

Additional Skills: Vocabulary (adjectives and nouns), Grammar

LEVEL:
2 to 4

GROUP:
3 or 4

10 to 15
MINUTES

MATERIALS & PREP WORK

Prepare two sets of cards. The first set has a different adjective written on each card with blue ink. The adjectives should be descriptive, such as *hard*, *soft*, *pretty*, *dry*, *wet*, and so on. You will need a set of 20 of these adjective cards for each group of students. The second set has a different noun written on each card with green ink. The nouns should be things, animals, food, and so on. You will need a set of at least five noun cards for each group.

THE GAME

The object of the game is come up with the most creative combination of an adjective and a noun. Some examples are "green egg," "flat cat," and "delicious car."

HOW TO PLAY

Give each group of students a set of adjective cards and a set of noun cards, and elect one person in each group to be the dealer. The dealer hands out five adjective cards to each group member. Then the dealer turns over one noun card and shows it to the group. The students in the group must select one adjective card from the five in their hand to pair with the noun. The students then need to use their adjective-noun combination in a sentence. For example, if the noun is *car,* and a student chooses the adjective *delicious*, he or she might say, "We made a cake in the shape of a car. It was the most delicious car in the world." The student with the most creative combination as decided by the players wins that round and takes the adjective and noun cards. Play continues as the next noun card is overturned. The student with the most pairs of cards at the end wins the game.

WHAT TO LOOK FOR

You'll know the game is working when the students can make sentences with the combinations of words they produced.

For higher-level classes, you could use this game to practice participial adjectives, like bored/boring, amused/amusing, and so on.

59

What's My Line?

Additional Skills: Vocabulary, Speaking, Listening

LEVEL:
2 to 4

GROUP:
4 or 5

🕐
20
MINUTES

MATERIALS & PREP WORK

This game offers a good review for vocabulary, such as occupations, fruit, animals, colors, and so on. Prepare a set of cards with a term belonging to one of the above categories written on each card. You will need one set for each group of students.

THE GAME

The object of the game is to guess the word written on a classmate's card by asking only yes-or-no questions.

HOW TO PLAY

Demonstrate the activity by drawing a card, for example, the word *waiter*. Say, "Try to guess this word by asking me questions. I can answer only yes or no. The category is occupations." Allow the students to ask you yes-or-no questions, such as "Do you work outside?" "Do you need any tools to do your job?" and "Do you do your job alone?" Once the students guess the word, have them sit with their partners, and hand out a set of cards to each group. One student draws a card and tells the group the category. The other students then try guessing the word written on the card by asking yes-or-no questions. The student who guesses correctly goes next.

WHAT TO LOOK FOR

Make sure the students are asking only yes-or-no questions. You'll know it's working when the students have gone through several cards.

For a wide variety of terms on your cards, stick with one category, like occupations, and dig deeper into its potential range of vocabulary.

60

Scattered Categories

Additional Skills: Vocabulary, Spelling

LEVEL:
2 to 5

GROUP:
3 or 4

🕐
10 to 15
MINUTES

MATERIALS & PREP WORK

Provide a set of letter dice (or you can find a number of free letter dice apps available for smartphones). Also prepare a list of potential categories, such as fruit, animals, foods, veggies, sports, and so on.

THE GAME

The object of the game is for students to work in groups to come up with a list of words beginning with a particular letter in a specific category.

HOW TO PLAY

Demonstrate the activity by writing one of the categories on the whiteboard—for example, "animals." Then roll the dice and write the letter that comes up, for example, the letter *F*. Appeal to the students for types of animals that begin with the letter *F*, such as frog, fish, ferret, and so on. Once the students get the idea, tell the students to work in their groups to roll the dice and come up with a list of words in the selected category that start with the letter rolled. At the appropriate time limit (one to two minutes), the group with the longest list of words gets the point for that round. Then change the category and play again.

WHAT TO LOOK FOR

You'll know it's working when the students are communicating with each other about the words they come up with and not just working alone.

For lower-level classes, you can roll two dice so that they have two letters with which to find a list of words.

Fancy Fairy Tales

61

Additional Skills: Vocabulary, Grammar, Listening, Speaking

LEVEL:
3 to 5

GROUP:
3 or 4

20 to 30
MINUTES

MATERIALS & PREP WORK

Prepare a short fairy tale, such as "Little Red Riding Hood." It should be a story with at least three or more characters. Make enough copies of the story for each student in the class.

THE GAME

The object of the game is for the students to work together to retell a fairy tale from the point of view of one of its characters. I like to use fairy tales for this activity because most students have a basic familiarity with the stories.

HOW TO PLAY

Hand out the story to each student and assign one of the characters to each group. For example, group 1 is Little Red Riding Hood, group 2 is the

Wolf, group 3 is Grandma, and so on. Give the students a few minutes to read through the story. Then tell each group to work together and rewrite the story from the point of view of the assigned character. You can help start them off with the following prompts:

1. Little Red Riding Hood: "Last Saturday I decided to take a walk through the woods to visit my grandmother."
2. The Wolf: "Last Saturday I was walking through the woods and feeling pretty hungry."
3. Grandma: "Last Saturday I was relaxing in my bed recovering from a bad cold."

WHAT TO LOOK FOR

You may need to suggest some ideas, such as "What did Little Red Riding Hood prepare to bring her grandmother?" or "What does the Wolf usually like to do on the weekends?"

I tell students to imagine this as animation, so they can add as much detail about the characters as they'd like.

62

Funniest Answer

Additional Skills: Vocabulary, Listening, Speaking.

LEVEL:
3 to 5

GROUP:
4 or 5

15 to 20
MINUTES

MATERIALS & PREP WORK

Prepare two sets of cards. The first set has a different question, like "What did I eat for dinner last night?" or statement, like "That shop has too many _____," on each card. You will need a set of 20 of these cards for each group. The other set has a different noun (either a word or a phrase), like *dogs*, *pink balloons*, or *pencils*, on each card. You will need a set of 20 of these cards for each group as well.

THE GAME

The goal is for the students to choose the funniest word to either answer the question or complete the statement.

HOW TO PLAY

For each group, place the question/statement cards facedown in the middle of the group. Then hand out four or five noun cards to each student. One person starts by drawing and reading a question/statement card. The other students choose one of their noun cards that they think would make the funniest match and hand that card to the reader. The reader then chooses one of the word cards and reads the sentence, filling in the "funny" word or supplying it as the answer to the question. When the laughter stops, the reader passes the statement card to the supplier of the funniest answer, and play continues with the next person. The person holding the most statement cards
at the end of the game is the winner.

WHAT TO LOOK FOR

You'll know it's working when there is a lot of laughter coming from the groups and they are getting in to using their imaginations.

To challenge higher-level groups, use more advanced vocabulary in the cards.

My Secret

63

Additional Skills: Vocabulary, Spelling

LEVEL:
3 to 5

GROUP:
4 or 5

🕐
**10 to 15
MINUTES**

MATERIALS & PREP WORK

Prepare a set of cards with an amusing or odd "secret" written on each—for example, "I fell asleep in my last English class," "I gave my teacher an apple with a worm in it," "I robbed a bank," or "I'm an accordion player." You will need one set for each group of students.

THE GAME

The object of the game is for the students to guess their classmate's "secret" by asking only yes-or-no questions.

HOW TO PLAY

For maximum fun and interaction, students work in groups of four or five. Give each group a set of cards, placed facedown. One student in the group is in the hot seat: He or she draws a card and cannot show it to the others. The rest of the group has to guess what the secret is by taking turns asking only yes-or-no questions. The student asking questions can continue until the student with the secret gives a "no" answer. At that point, the next student begins posing questions. The person who correctly guesses the secret is the winner of that round. Play continues for four to five minutes per round maximum; if nobody can guess the secret before time is up, the student can reveal it, and the next person draws a card.

WHAT TO LOOK FOR

Make sure that students are asking only yes-or-no questions, as this is the key to the game.

Feel free to vary the types of "secrets" you write on the cards, depending on the interests and level of your class.

Question Me

64

Additional Skills: Vocabulary, Questions

LEVEL:
3 to 5

GROUP:
4 or 5

**10
MINUTES**

MATERIALS & PREP WORK

Prepare a list of vocabulary learned during the class or the week.

THE GAME

The object of the game is to review vocabulary in a fun and creative way with your class.

HOW TO PLAY

This is an end-of-class, *Jeopardy*-style game to review vocabulary learned during a lesson. Demonstrate first by writing one of the words on the board. The teams have to formulate a question or statement to which this word is the answer. For example, if you write the word *bored*, the students could come up with a statement like "How I feel when I watch golf on TV." The first group to come up with a correct statement or question referring to the word wins the point.

WHAT TO LOOK FOR

Observe the groups to make sure that they are working and communicating together to come up with a correct statement.

If you like, this game can be played with a specific list of vocabulary words, phrasal verbs, or even idioms.

Spelling & Number Games

Did You Write It Right?

Additional Skills: Spelling, Vocabulary

MATERIALS & PREP WORK

Prepare a worksheet with illustrations of one item each from sets of homonyms, like brake/break, cereal/serial, flu/flew, for/four, foul/fowl, hair/hare, heal/heel, mail/male, minor/miner, peace/piece, principal/principle, red/read, stationary/stationery, through/threw, toe/tow, waist/waste, where/ware/wear, and wood/would. The homonyms should also be written underneath each picture. Make enough copies of the worksheet for each group in your class.

THE GAME

This activity focuses on identifying homonyms. These can be very tricky for English learners because they sound alike yet have different spellings. The worksheet presents common pairs of homonyms along with an illustration of one of the words.

HOW TO PLAY

Write the following two sentences on the board: "This is the book I read last night," and "The colors of a stop sign are white and red." Then ask the students to read each sentence. Next, circle the words *read* and *red*. Ask the students to read those words aloud, tell them that *read* and *red* are homonyms, and write the word *homonyms* on the board. Then hand out one worksheet to each group. Tell the students to look at each illustration and the words below it. They are to decide as a group which is the correct spelling that matches the picture and circle it. The group with the most correct choices is the winner.

WHAT TO LOOK FOR

You can allow lower-level groups to use their English-language dictionaries if you feel they need help.

Download a free worksheet for this game at callistomediabooks.com/esl-games.

66

Word List Race

Additional Skills: Spelling, Vocabulary

LEVEL:
1 to 3

GROUP:
3 or 4

10 to 15 MINUTES

MATERIALS & PREP WORK

Prepare cards with commonly used letter combinations, for example, *th, nt, ly,* and *er.* Make enough so there is a different card for each group.

THE GAME

The object of the game is for students to come up with a list of words based on a common two-letter combination.

HOW TO PLAY

Give each group one card. Tell the students they have two minutes to write down as many words as they can think of using the letter combination they have received. When the buzzer rings, tell the groups to stop writing and to pass their card to another group. Then put another two minutes on the clock. Repeat this process until all the teams have made a list with each card. At the end of the activity, the team with the most words wins.

WHAT TO LOOK FOR

You'll want to make sure the students are working together to come up with the group's list of words, not just writing their own list in silence.

You can vary the types of letters on the cards as you like. For example, you might include repeated letters (*tt, pp, rr, ee*) or three-letter combinations instead of just two.

67

A Kind Elephant

Additional Skills: Spelling, Vocabulary

LEVEL:
1 to 5

GROUP:
3 or 4

10 to 15 MINUTES

MATERIALS & PREP WORK

None.

THE GAME

The object of the game is to rearrange letters in a sentence to form other words. Higher-level students should form other sentences instead of words. While helping students use vocabulary they may have learned but do not use on a daily basis, this game also helps students work on spelling English words that can be tricky for those from other countries.

HOW TO PLAY

Write the key sentence on the whiteboard, "A kind elephant at the zoo ate very interesting peanuts." For lower-level students, tell the class that many words are hiding in this sentence. Then, circle several letters in the sentence and write a word with those letters. For example, circle *A, l, p, e,* and *p,* then write *Apple*. Say, "Now it's your turn. How many words can you find? Work with your partners. You have 10 minutes."

For higher-level students, tell the class that many words are hiding in this sentence and that those words can form another sentence. Point to the letters and write the sentence "Apes play tennis." Then say, "Now it's your turn. How many sentences can you find? Work with your partners. You have 15 minutes." When the time is up, ask each group to report one or two of their words/sentences to the class.

WHAT TO LOOK FOR

Make sure the students are talking to each other. You can facilitate this by having key phrases on the board, like "I found *Apes*" and "What word did you find?"

Feel free to substitute your own key sentence; just make sure you use a wide enough variety of letters. You can also make the activity more challenging by restricting the doubling of letters. The key sentence above, for example, has 2 *p*'s and several *t*'s but only one *g*, so the students can create words like *apple* or *pattern* but not *giggle*.

First Two/Last Two

68

Additional Skills: Spelling, Vocabulary

★
LEVEL:
1 to 5

GROUP:
3 or 4

🕐
10 to 15
MINUTES

MATERIALS & PREP WORK

None.

THE GAME

The object of the game is to come up with a list of words based on the first two or last two letters of a word written on the whiteboard.

HOW TO PLAY

Demonstrate how the game works by asking the group for the name of an animal—for example, *tiger.* Circle the last two letters and ask the students to call out words that either end or begin with the same two last letters (*er*), and write those words on the board. Once the students get the idea, the game can begin. Write the word *lion* on the board. Students work together in their groups to write as many words as possible that start or end with the last two letters as *lion*—that is, *on* (such as *only* or *passion*). Set the timer for one minute. At the end of this period, the team with the longest list of words gets the point.

WHAT TO LOOK FOR

This should be a communicative activity for the students, so make sure they are interacting and not just writing in silence.

One variation is to use both the first two letters and the last two letters of the target word. So for the word *lion*, the students need to come up with words that begin with *li* (*live*, *lip*, etc.) or words that end with *on*.

69

Silly Tongue Twisters

LEVEL:
2 to 5

GROUP:
3 or 4

🕐
10 to 15
MINUTES

Additional Skills: Spelling, Vocabulary

MATERIALS & PREP WORK

Prepare a handout with a list of target minimal pairs that you want your students to practice, for example, seat/sheet, sore/shore, sip/ship, sign/shine, sort/short, suit/shoot, save/shave, gas/gash, mess/mesh, mass/mash, fist/fished, last/lashed, sock/shock, and sea/she.

THE GAME

The object of the game is for the students to come up with an original tongue twister they can use to practice minimal pairs.

HOW TO PLAY

Tongue twisters (like "She sells sea shells by the seashore") provide a great way to practice pronunciation, especially with minimal pairs. In this game, students compete in groups to create the most original tongue twister. Give each group a handout and decide on a time limit, such as 10 minutes. Tell each group to work together to write its own tongue twister featuring the handout's list of words. Of course, students are free to use other words as well. Award a point (or, for greater incentive, a prize) to the group that includes the most minimal pairs in the tongue twister it produces.

WHAT TO LOOK FOR

Students may need help coming up with "filler" words to round out their tongue twisters, so be ready to help them out. They will also need to practice reading their final product.

At the end of the activity, have each group perform a reading of its tongue twister for the rest of the class.

Prefix Opposites

Additional Skills: Spelling, Vocabulary

LEVEL:
3 to 5

GROUP:
3 or 4

🕐

**10 to 15
MINUTES**

MATERIALS & PREP WORK

Prepare a handout with a list of adjectives whose opposites can be formed by using the prefixes *dis-*, *il-*, *im-*, *in-*, *ir-*, and *un-*.

THE GAME

The object of the game is for small groups of students to come up with a list of adjectives whose opposites can be formed by using the prefixes.

HOW TO PLAY

Give one handout to each student, and have them sit in groups of three or four. On the board, write the prefixes *dis-*, *il-*, *im-*, *in-*, *ir-*, and *un-*, and elicit from the class one adjective starting with each of those prefixes. Then tell the students that they need to work with their partners to list adjectives that form their opposite by using one of these prefixes. The group that produces the most correct opposite adjectives will be the winner.

WHAT TO LOOK FOR

Some students may be confused about whether a word uses *il-* or *ir-*, and *im-* or *in-*, so you may need to assist if that happens.

For more advanced students, you may want to require that they write a sentence for each adjective they come up with.

Suffix Challenge

71

Additional Skills: Spelling, Vocabulary

LEVEL:
3 to 5

GROUP:
2 or 3

**10
MINUTES**

MATERIALS & PREP WORK

None.

THE GAME

The object of the game is for students to come up with a list of words that use a particular set of suffixes.

HOW TO PLAY

Write a list of common suffixes on the board, for example, *-able, -full, -ment, -sion, -tion, -ive*, and so on. Demonstrate the activity by asking the class for words that end in each of those suffixes, and write them on the board. Tell the students they will have 10 minutes to make a list of as many words ending in those suffixes as they can. The pair or group with the most words is the winner.

WHAT TO LOOK FOR

Lower-level students may need a little help distinguishing the spelling of -*sion* and -*tion* words.

> You can also limit this activity to words with just one or two suffixes, or to just nouns or adjectives, depending on the abilities of your class.

72

Say the Number

Additional Skills: Numbers (large numbers), Speaking

LEVEL:
1 to 3

GROUP:
5 or 6

🕐

5 to 10
MINUTES

MATERIALS & PREP WORK

Provide five or six oversize foam dice or download a tablet app that can generate a random number (e.g., the Random Number Generator).

THE GAME

The object of the game is to be the first team to call out a large number when it appears on the dice or tablet.

HOW TO PLAY

This game works best with actual oversize foam dice, but you can still achieve the same purpose with a random-number app on a tablet. Roll four or five dice, one at a time. Each die represents one digit in a large number. So if you roll 3, 4, 1, the students need to call out, "Three hundred forty-one." The first team to call out the number gets the point. Continue rolling until one team reaches 20 points.

WHAT TO LOOK FOR

Monitor the activity from the front of the room, and assist the students as necessary.

> If you have a tablet and a projector available, you can play this game without actual dice.

Big Number Bingo

Additional Skills: Numbers, Reading, Listening

LEVEL:
1 to 3

GROUP:
2

10 MINUTES

MATERIALS & PREP WORK

Prepare bingo boards with a five-by-five grid, and in each space write a three-, four-, or five-digit number. Vary the positions of the numbers on the board, and make each board a bit different. You'll need at least two different boards for each group. You'll also need a list of the numbers in random order.

THE GAME

Large numbers are a challenge for many students. The object of the game is for the students to listen for the number being called out and to find it on the bingo board.

HOW TO PLAY

Give one bingo board to each pair of students. In case some students are not familiar with the game of bingo, demonstrate how it works. Tell the students that you will say each number only one time, so they will need to listen carefully. Make sure that you read the numbers consistently. For example, you could read 432 as "four hundred and thirty-two" or "four hundred thirty-two." The first team to get bingo is the winner. Then, hand out a second bingo board to the groups and start again.

WHAT TO LOOK FOR

As this is a pairs activity, it's a good idea to keep an eye and an ear on each pair of students to make sure they are working together, as opposed to one student marking all the answers.

If the level of your class is more advanced, you could make this activity more challenging by preparing bingo cards with similar-sounding numbers, for example, 24,636 and 24,363.

Number Dictation

74

Additional Skills: Numbers, Listening

LEVEL:
1 to 3

GROUP:
2 or 3

🕐
10 to 15
MINUTES

MATERIALS & PREP WORK

Prepare a list of 15 to 20 sentences that each contain a large number. Examples include "The pet shop has 2,363 fish" and "A new Ford costs $28,978."

THE GAME

The object of the game is for students to work together to listen for and then write down large numbers.

HOW TO PLAY

Model the activity by telling the students to listen for the numbers in the following sentence: "As of 2018, there are over 1,700 parks in New York City."

Explain that you're going to read them some additional sentences containing numbers for them to attempt to write down. Make it clear that you're going to read each sentence only one time. After you read each sentence, they will need to work with their partners to see if the group can come up with the correct sentence, including any numbers they contain.

WHAT TO LOOK FOR

Monitor the groups to make sure that they are communicating in English about what they heard and not just showing their partners the sentence they wrote.

Vary the length of the numbers depending on the level of your students. For a lower-level class, you may consider reading just numbers rather than entire sentences.

The Price Is Right

75

Additional Skills: Numbers (prices)

LEVEL:
1 to 3

GROUP:
3 or 4

10 to 15
MINUTES

MATERIALS & PREP WORK

Get a sale flyer from your local supermarket. Many supermarkets now make these flyers available online, and if not, they are usually available at the entrance to the store. Either cover the prices of some items with Post-it notes or prepare photos of the items themselves.

THE GAME

The object of the game is for students to guess the price of everyday items at the grocery store.

HOW TO PLAY

Demonstrate the game by showing the students one item from the flyer. Ask them to work with their partners to try to estimate the price of that item without going over. Once the students get the idea, tell them the game will begin, and they will have 30 seconds to discuss possible prices with their group. The group that comes closest to the actual price in the supermarket flyer without going over wins a point. You can then continue to the next item.

WHAT TO LOOK FOR

Monitor the groups from the front of the classroom to make sure they are communicating with each other about the possible price for each item.

For lower-level classes, you may want to review and practice English pronunciation of different amounts of money.

Did You Catch That?

76

Additional Skills: Numbers, Listening, Speaking

LEVEL:
3 to 5

GROUP:
3 or 4

10 to 15
MINUTES

MATERIALS & PREP WORK

Find a recording of a traffic report from your local TV or radio station. The AM radio stations broadcast these frequently in the mornings.

THE GAME

In this game, students listen to a traffic report to identify the numbers spoken during the short broadcast. This activity works best when the traffic report is from your local area, as the students may be more familiar with the local roads.

HOW TO PLAY

Ask your students for some examples of numbers related to the traffic and transit in the area, for example, Route 66, 40 miles per hour, the CT 3 bus, and so on. Quite often the traffic reports mention the time as well. As a class, have a conversation about the busiest roads, train lines, bus routes, and so on in your town. This will help get some of the vocabulary from the broadcast into their heads. Then tell the students they are going to listen to a traffic report (a recording from radio or TV). They will need to work with their partners to write down all of the numbers they hear during that broadcast. Play the recording no more than three times, and then have the groups share their results.

WHAT TO LOOK FOR

You'll want to make sure that the students are communicating with each other to collectively come up with the list of numbers.

For lower-level classes, you can prepare a handout with the numbers from the report plus other similar numbers, then have the students circle the numbers they hear.

Grammar
Games

The Great Adjective Divide

Additional Skills: Grammar (comparative adjectives), Vocabulary, Spelling

MATERIALS & PREP WORK

Prepare a handout with a mixed list of adjectives in these three categories: One syllable, more than one syllable, and those ending in the letter y.

THE GAME

This object of this game is to break down the three forms of comparative adjectives.

HOW TO PLAY

The comparative form of an adjective is determined by two factors: syllable count and spelling. Generally, when the adjective is one syllable, the comparative form is made by adding -er, as in *taller* or *older*. For adjectives containing two or more syllables, we place the word *more* before the adjective, as in *more expensive* or *more interesting*. For adjectives ending in *y*, we change the *y* to *i* and add -er, as in *prettier* or *happier*. Distribute the handout and tell the students they need to work with their partners to divide the adjectives into three groups. Do not tell them what the groups are. This activity provides a good introduction to this grammar point.

WHAT TO LOOK FOR

For groups that finish quickly, have the students practice writing sentences with the words.

> You may want to give lower-level students a hint. For example, tell them that some adjectives take -er while others take *more*.

Get in Line

Additional Skills: Grammar (comparatives and superlatives), Listening, Speaking

★

LEVEL:
1 to 3

GROUP:
5 or 6

🕐
10 to 15
MINUTES

MATERIALS & PREP WORK

Prepare cards with different animal names written on them, providing at least one animal card per student.

THE GAME

This activity is for students to practice comparatives and superlatives in a meaningful and conversational way. Students will need to listen, speak, and cooperate with one another.

HOW TO PLAY

Give each student a card with the name of an animal written on it (cat, snake, lion, frog, etc.). Write one criterion on the board, for example, "speed." The students then must work together to determine which animal is the fastest, second fastest, and so on, all the way down to the slowest, and line them up in that order. The group that finishes first gets the point. Examine the group's work to see if it was done correctly; then write the next criterion on the board. Examples might include height, weight, length, cuteness, and so on.

WHAT TO LOOK FOR

Make sure the students are using the target language to determine the order in which the animals line up.

As a challenge to higher levels, ask the groups to come up with their own criteria for lining up the animals.

At, On, In

79

Additional Skills: Grammar
(prepositions of time), Listening

LEVEL:
1 to 3

GROUP:
5 or 6

🕐

**5 to 10
MINUTES**

MATERIALS & PREP WORK

Create big cards with *AT*, *ON*, and *IN* written on
them, respectively, as large as possible. You will
need one set of cards for each group. Then make
a list of phrases regarding time that go with *at*, *on*,
and *in*. There should be at least 8 to 10 phrases
to match each preposition.

THE GAME

The object of this game is to drill usage of the three
prepositions of time. Many students mix up which
prepositions go with which time phrase. Remember that *at* is used with clock time, *on* with a day or
date, and *in* with everything else. Special cases are
"*at* night" and "*on* the weekend."

HOW TO PLAY

Divide the class into teams. Each team can have
a name, so write those team names on the board.
The teams score a point every time they answer
correctly. Give each team one set of cards with
the prepositions *AT*, *ON*, and *IN* written on them.

To demonstrate, say, "Nine o'clock," then hold up the *AT* card and say, "At nine o'clock." The students should catch on pretty quickly how the game works. Just tell the students that all team members need to agree on the answer before the team gives its response.

Call out a word, which is either clock time (nine o'clock, noon, midnight, etc. used with *at*), a day (Valentine's Day, Tuesday, June 3rd, etc. used with *on*), or another time word (the 1990s, spring, the 18th century, etc. used with *in*). Teams need to decide which preposition matches which word, and one person from each team holds up the card that provides the correct preposition.

WHAT TO LOOK FOR

Since this is a team effort, the team members should consult with each other before giving the answer. If you say "June third" and one student blurts out "On June third" without consulting his or her teammates, the team doesn't get the point.

You can vary this game by having the students write their answers instead of speaking them out loud. In this case you don't need to prepare the cards. After the game, the groups check their answers, and the team with the most correct answers wins.

80

How's Your Memory?

Additional Skills: Grammar (prepositions),
Writing, Vocabulary

LEVEL:
1 to 3

GROUP:
2 or 3

10 to 15
MINUTES

MATERIALS & PREP WORK

Prepare a photo of a messy room. Search Google
Images for "messy college student's bedroom
background."

THE GAME

The object of the game is for students to look at
a picture, notice what it contains and where these
things are located, then write as many sentences
as they can to describe it.

HOW TO PLAY

Demonstrate this game by using your desk and
objects on it as an example. Prompt statements
from the students, such as, "There is a laptop on
the desk" or "There are some books next to the

laptop." Either show the photo you've prepared on a projector or hand out a copy to each student. If you hand it out, ask the students to keep it facedown on their desk until you give the signal. Let the students look at the picture for three minutes. Then, have the students write as many sentences as possible describing from memory where everything is located in the room, for example, "The laptop is on the desk" and "The speaker is on the desk between the lamp and the laptop."

WHAT TO LOOK FOR

Make sure the students aren't looking at the picture once the time is up.

You may want to give the groups a time limit to write their sentences. The students could also elect one member of their group to be the scribe to write the sentences and then check the sentences afterward with their classmates.

Comparative Race

81

Additional Skills: Grammar (comparative adjectives), Vocabulary

★
LEVEL:
1 to 3

👤
GROUP:
2 or 3

🕐
10 to 15
MINUTES

MATERIALS & PREP WORK

None

THE GAME

In this game, pairs or groups of students receive two items to compare. The object is to use these items to practice forming comparative sentences and to use this grammar point in a conversational manner.

HOW TO PLAY

Elicit two examples in the same category (cities, fruit, sports, etc.) from the students and write them on the board—for example, New York and Chicago, apples and grapes, or golf and baseball. Each pair or group of students must then work together to try to come up with the most comparative sentences for the word pair. Examples include "Apples are bigger than grapes," "Grapes are lighter than apples," "Grapes are more expensive than apples," and so on. The team that creates the most sentences for the word pair is the winner. Then, choose another pair of words, and repeat the exercise.

WHAT TO LOOK FOR

The sentences should be sensible and factual to the extent of the students' knowledge. For example, it's hard to know if grapes are more expensive than apples, but if the grammar is okay, then I would accept the sentence.

Setting a time limit puts productive pressure on the groups. For lower-level groups, you may want to elicit a list of adjectives and include those on the board before the game begins.

For or Since

Additional Skills: Grammar (present perfect tense and for/since)

LEVEL:
1 to 3

GROUP:
DIVIDE THE
CLASS INTO
TWO TEAMS

10 to 15
MINUTES

MATERIALS & PREP WORK

Prepare two lists of time phrases. One is a list of particular points in time (these are preceded by *since*). The other is a list of time periods (these are preceded by *for*).

THE GAME

The object of the game is for students to use the correct preposition based on the time phrases prompted by the teacher.

HOW TO PLAY

Divide the class in half to make two teams. Write the words *for* and *since* on the board. Ask the students for one present perfect sentence for each word and write both on the board—for example, "I have been here for two months" and

"I have been here since February." Circle the phrases *for two months* and *since February*. Tell the class that you are going to offer some other phrases like these using *for* and *since*. When you do, the students have to make a correct sentence including your phrase. For example, if you say, "Three months," and a student says, "I've been studying English here for three months," that student's team gets the point, and play continues.

WHAT TO LOOK FOR

Since this is a group activity, encourage all students to try to answer, and ask the more dominating students to give their classmates a chance.

As a variation, instead of playing in teams, you could have the students write their sentences individually at their desks. Then, at the end of the activity, have them provide the class with an example of what they wrote.

It's Sporty

Additional Skills: Grammar (verbs, go + -ing), Vocabulary

LEVEL:
1 to 3

GROUP:
3

10 to 15
MINUTES

MATERIALS & PREP WORK

Prepare a worksheet with a mixed list of sports in each of three categories: those that use *play* (sports that are nouns and use a ball or ball-like object—e.g., baseball, badminton, etc.), those that use *do* (sports that are nouns but don't have a ball—e.g., yoga, fencing, etc.), and those that use *go* (sports that are spelled with -*ing*—e.g., skiing, swimming, etc.). Write the list of sports in the top third of the worksheet. Use the lower two thirds to draw three large boxes or circles.

THE GAME

The object of the game is for the students to discover the three categories of sports and practice their correct usage. Don't tell the students about the categories at all. The point of this exercise is to see if the students can guess what the three categories are.

HOW TO PLAY

Play this game in two parts. Part 1: Hand out a copy of the worksheet to each student. Tell the students that they will have five minutes or so to divide the list into three groups. It's up to the students to decide with their partners how they define the groups. Part 2: When time is up, have a mixer. Tell the students to change partners and work in a new group of three. Ask them to exchange their ideas with their new partners, and then after a few minutes, stop the activity and see if any of the groups have come up with the correct answer for this exercise.

WHAT TO LOOK FOR

Make sure the students are communicating with each other during this exercise and not just working silently.

For lower-level students, you may want to skip part 2 and just review the students' ideas as a class.

Make 'Em Say It

Additional Skills: Grammar (frequency adverbs), Listening, Speaking

LEVEL:
1 to 3

GROUP:
2

10 to 15 MINUTES

MATERIALS & PREP WORK

Prepare a set of cards with five frequency adverbs (*always, usually, sometimes, hardly ever, never*). You will need one set of cards for each pair of students in your class.

THE GAME

In this game, students provide clues to prompt their partner to create a sentence using frequency adverbs.

HOW TO PLAY

To demonstrate this activity, write the five frequency adverbs on the board. Give one student a clue. For example, say, "You do this with your hands before you eat something." The goal is for the student to reply something like, "I always wash my hands before eating." Then have the students sit in pairs. Give one student in each pair a set of cards, and ask him or her to mix up the cards and pick one. That student needs to give clues or ask a question to motivate his or her partner to answer using the selected frequency adverb. Once all of these adverbs have been used in a response, each pair can change roles.

WHAT TO LOOK FOR

Some of the lower-level students may need help coming up with clues or questions for their partners.

A variation of this game would be to create a card offering suggestions for some common and uncommon activities, like "wash your hands" or "go to the beach in the winter." Students can use frequency adverbs and other clues to motivate their partners to guess the activity.

85

Not Regular Bingo

Additional Skills: Grammar (past participles), Listening

LEVEL:
1 to 3

GROUP:
3 or 4

10 to 15
MINUTES

MATERIALS & PREP WORK

Prepare bingo boards with a five-by-five grid containing the past participle form of 25 irregular verbs, such as *gone, eaten, brought,* and *frozen.* Each bingo board should have a different layout of the words or at least some variety. You will need at least one bingo board for each group of students.

THE GAME

The object of the game is for students to practice identifying the past participle of irregular verbs in English.

HOW TO PLAY

You can warm up for this activity by calling out a few verbs and asking the students to respond with the past participle form. When you do this, include a mix of regular and irregular verbs. Then hand out one bingo board to each group. Tell the students that you are going to call out the present form of the verb and that, as a group, they need to decide upon the past participle form of that verb and mark the bingo card appropriately. The first group to get bingo is the winner. You could also continue the game with another set of words and/or bingo boards.

WHAT TO LOOK FOR

Look around the room and monitor the groups to make sure all the students are working together to mark the bingo cards.

For a variation of this game, you could substitute adjectives for irregular verbs and make this an "opposite" bingo game. For example, you could make bingo boards using adjectives (such as *expensive*, *small*, and *old*), then call out other adjectives with the opposite meaning to those on the board (such as *cheap*, *big*, and *young*).

86

What Is/Was Going On?

★
LEVEL:
1 to 3

GROUP:
2 or 3

🕐
10
MINUTES

Additional Skills: Grammar (past continuous, present continuous), Speaking, Listening

MATERIALS & PREP WORK

Prepare an image of a busy street scene. To locate examples, do a Google Image search for "busy street scene cartoon."

THE GAME

The object of the game is to remember as many people's actions as possible in a busy street scene and to write them down using the correct tense.

HOW TO PLAY

You can either show the image on a projector or hand out copies of it. In either case, let the students look at the image for three minutes. Then give the groups four to five minutes to write down from memory what all of the people in the picture either are doing (to practice the present continuous tense) or were doing (to practice the past continuous tense). The group with the most sentences wins.

WHAT TO LOOK FOR

You'll want to make sure the students are speaking with their partners to come up with the list together and not just working silently on their own.

For higher-level students, you could ask them to write more complicated sentences—for example, explaining the reason that a person in the picture is or was doing something in particular.

An Educated Guess

Additional Skills: Grammar (modals of probability: must, probably, may, might, can't, etc.)

LEVEL:
2 to 3

GROUP:
2

5 to 10 MINUTES

MATERIALS & PREP WORK

Prepare an image of a teenager's bedroom. You can search Google Images for "teenager's bedroom with the bed unmade." You can show this picture on a projector or make a copy for each pair of students.

THE GAME

The object of the game is for students to guess the teenager's lifestyle based on the picture of the bedroom while using the target language in a meaningful way.

HOW TO PLAY

Show your students the picture on the projector or hand out a copy to each pair. Ask the class a question based on the picture—for example,

"Based on this photo, what kind of music do you think he likes?" The goal is to elicit answers like, "He must like rock and roll" or "He probably doesn't like hip-hop."

Then, tell the students, "Now it's your turn. Work with your partner to ask and respond to questions like this. You have 10 minutes."

At the end of the activity, have the pairs report some of their findings to the class.

WHAT TO LOOK FOR

Make sure the students are asking and responding to each other's questions. For lower-level students, you may need to prompt them with suggestions, like "Vic, ask Jen about music."

To reinforce the language skills practiced, you can ask the pairs to write down their answers, especially the lower-level students. For higher-level students, you might ask them to compare themselves to the teenager in their response, such as "He must like rock music. I do, too!"

Back to the Future

Additional Skills: Grammar (verb tenses/the future), Vocabulary

LEVEL:
2 to 4

GROUP:
2 or 3

10 to 15
MINUTES

MATERIALS & PREP WORK

Prepare a few handouts with some short stories, like fairy tales or other children's stories. You will need one handout for each group in your class; ideally each group should have a different story.

THE GAME

The object of the game is to rewrite a story from past to future tense. In doing so, students will need to get a little creative regarding which future tense they choose, along with which related vocabulary.

HOW TO PLAY

Write a few sentences about what you did last weekend. For example, "I woke up late. After

breakfast, I went to the mall since I wanted to buy new shoes."
Then, elicit from the class the future version of your sentences.
You'll get something like this: "I am going to wake up late. After
eating breakfast, I will go to the mall since I want to buy new
shoes." Once the students get the idea, hand out the stories.
Tell them that they will have 10 to 15 minutes to change the
story from the past to the future.

WHAT TO LOOK FOR

Make sure the students are talking to each other and not just
writing this by themselves.

> For more advanced students, you might ask them to
> change the ending of the story, for example, "The big, bad
> wolf thinks he will eat Grandma, but she is going to chase
> him away."

89

Because . . .

Additional Skills: Grammar (conjunctions), Speaking, Listening

LEVEL:
2 to 4

GROUP:
3 or 4

10 to 15
MINUTES

MATERIALS & PREP WORK

Prepare a set of cards with one statement per card. Each statement represents the second half of a sentence that starts with either "Because . . ." (for example, "I'm so full" or "I need to buy milk") or "Because of . . ." (such as "we canceled the picnic"). Prepare enough statement cards so that each group will have 10 to 15 cards. About half of each set should match with *because* and the other half with *because of.*

THE GAME

The intent of this game is to help students distinguish between the forms of *because* and *because of* in a fun, competitive format.

HOW TO PLAY

Each group gets a set of cards facedown. The first student draws a card from the deck and reads the statement. The other group members then race to put down a phrase starting with "Because ..." or "Because of ..." that creates a good match with the other half of the sentence. For example, the first student reads, "I'm so full," so another student might come up with "Because I ate so much pizza, I'm so full." The student who answers first keeps the card. In the end, the student with the most cards (i.e., the quickest answers) is the winner.

WHAT TO LOOK FOR

The student answering must make a complete sentence that begins with "Because ..." or "Because of ..." and ends with the phrase written on the card.

> This game can be adapted to other grammar points, such as conditionals, transitions (*despite, in spite of, even though, although, during, while*), and so on.

Draw the Scene

Additional Skills: Grammar (prepositions of location), Listening, Speaking

LEVEL:
2 to 4

GROUP:
4 or 5

10 to 15
MINUTES

MATERIALS & PREP WORK

Prepare several pictures from a magazine, such as different images of a house and yard.

THE GAME

In this interactive game, a student holding a picture must describe the image using prepositions of location and other vocabulary while the other students attempt to draw this image based on that description.

HOW TO PLAY

You can demonstrate this activity by showing a picture to the whole class. Make it clear where things are in the picture. For example, say, "This is a small house. There is a garage and driveway on the right side of the house. In the driveway is a small car. There is a big tree on the left side of the driveway."

Have students sit in their groups, and hand out one picture to one student in each group, making sure the other members of the group do not see the picture. The student who is holding the picture should describe it and where each element is located in the picture. The other classmates in the group then make drawings based on that student's description. At the end of the activity, students vote on the drawing that most closely matches the original picture.

WHAT TO LOOK FOR

Check whether the students doing the drawing are asking the student with the picture questions. You can decide whether or not to permit this.

Future Me

Additional Skills: Grammar (future tense), Listening, Speaking

LEVEL:
2 to 4

**GROUP:
WHOLE
CLASS**

**10 to 15
MINUTES**

MATERIALS & PREP WORK

Prepare a handout with six future-tense sentences, such as the following:

1. After class I will/I am going to

   _____.

2. Tomorrow morning I will/I am going to

   _____.

3. For my next vacation I will/I am going to

   _____.

4. _____ I will/I am going to have my hair cut.

5. I will/I am going to _____ in a year from now.

6. Someday, I will/I am going to live

   _____.

THE GAME

The object of this game is to practice future tenses ("will" and/or "am going to") and to ask and answer questions about another's future plans and activities.

HOW TO PLAY

Distribute a copy of the handout to each student, and give the class a few minutes to complete the sentences. Make sure the students understand that *will* is used when we have a guess about the future and *am going to* is used when we have a plan in the future. When the students have completed the questions, have a mixer. Ask the students to stand up with their papers, find a partner, and ask each other about their future selves. For example, one student asks, "What are you going to do after class?" The partner replies, "Maybe I will do some homework. How about you?" The first student says, "I am going to go to work. I have a part-time job." After a few minutes, stop the activity. Ask the students to find new partners and repeat the practice.

WHAT TO LOOK FOR

Make sure that the students are on task, asking and answering questions in full sentences.

> For a variation of this game, after the first round, ask the students to find new partners. This time they need to tell the new partner what their old partner's future self is going to do.

Mixed-Up Schedules

Additional Skills: Grammar (prepositions of time and place), Listening, Speaking

LEVEL:
2 to 4

GROUP:
WHOLE
CLASS

10 to 15
MINUTES

MATERIALS & PREP WORK

Prepare a page from the weekly schedule of "the boss" of a company. This boss is a very busy person with 12 to 15 different appointments at assorted times and days throughout the week. Make four variations of this schedule. For each one, white out three or four of the appointments (the time, the person the boss is meeting, the place, etc.). Each student will receive one of these variations.

THE GAME

The object of the game is for students to complete the missing information in the particular version of the schedule they have been given.

HOW TO PLAY

This is a mixer activity, so the students will need to stand up. Hand out the schedules to the students and tell them to take a look. Some of the information is missing, so they will need to walk around the room and try to find someone who has the information they need. Similarly, they will be able to provide some information needed by their classmates. The key point is that the students are not allowed to show their schedules to their classmates—they must use their language skills to complete the task instead.

WHAT TO LOOK FOR

Make sure that the students are using the target language to ask and answer questions.

This game could also be played as a pairs activity. In this case, just create two variations of the original schedule.

93

An Old-Fashioned Postcard

LEVEL:
2 to 5

GROUP:
2

10 MINUTES

Additional Skills: Grammar (past tense, present perfect tense, future tense), Vocabulary, Writing

MATERIALS & PREP WORK

For this game you will need some touristy postcards from your city. You can play this with real postcards if you happen to live in a city that has lots of cheap souvenir shops. If not, any photo of your city will do, and the students can use the back of the photo to write.

You will also need a set of different character cards, one for each student, containing three descriptive items: the character's name, age, and gender.

THE GAME

The object of this activity is for students use their imagination to write a story of how their character spent the past two days in your city. The story should be based on the age and gender of the character.

HOW TO PLAY

Hand out one character card and one postcard to each student. As an example, take one character card and read it aloud. "I'm Kim. I'm a 17-year-old girl." Then pick up a postcard. Pantomime writing on the card and say, "I've had fun in New York, but the past two days have been so busy. I arrived on Friday with my mom. After checking in, we went shopping." Then, tell the students that it's their turn to look at their character card and write a corresponding story for their character on their postcard. At the end of the activity, they can each read their card to their partner.

WHAT TO LOOK FOR

If the students seem stuck, give them hints about topics they can write about—famous places they visited, where they shopped, what they bought, what types of food they ate, and so on.

At the end of the exercise, you can have the students work in small groups of three or four. One student reads his or her card, and the others in the group can ask follow-up questions, like "Were you bored at the museum?" or "How was the pizza?"

★
LEVEL:
2 to 5

GROUP:
4 or 5

🕐
10 to 15
MINUTES

Best Advice

Additional Skills: Grammar (modals of necessity: Must, have to, need to, should, ought to, had better; third conditional: "If I were you, I would . . ."), Listening, Speaking

MATERIALS & PREP WORK

Prepare a set of cards that describe problems or situations needing advice, such as "I need to lose weight"; "I am having boyfriend/girlfriend problems"; "I want to have a pet, but I can't decide which one to get"; and so on. You'll need one set of cards for each group.

THE GAME

The object of the game is for one student to present a problem to the group and solicit advice for it.

HOW TO PLAY

In each group, one student draws a card and reads it. The other students have one minute to write down their advice. The first student then reads the problem card again, and the other students read their advice. The first student decides which is the best advice and hands the card to the person who gave it. Then the next student in the group draws a problem card and reads it, and play continues. The student who has collected the most cards (i.e., gave the best advice the most often) by the end of the game is the winner.

WHAT TO LOOK FOR

Make sure that the students giving advice are using complete sentences and include the target grammar point. For example, the advice should be "You should get a cat" and not "Get a cat."

For higher-level students, you might hand out cards with business problems, such as "Our company needs to increase sales," or governmental problems, like, "We need to build a new library in town."

95

Conditional Concentration

LEVEL:
2 to 5

GROUP:
3 or 4

10 to 15
MINUTES

Additional Skills: Grammar (conditional sentences)

MATERIALS & PREP WORK

Prepare a list of 10 conditional sentences containing an *if* clause—for example, "If it rains tomorrow, I will bring my umbrella." Write the *if* clauses from the sentences on one set of cards and the other half of the sentences on another set of cards. Each group will need both sets.

THE GAME

The object of the game is to match two halves of a sentence containing an *if* clause. As in the classic concentration game, players need to remember which cards contain a matching pair of clauses. Students take turns turning over two cards at a time to try to find a match.

HOW TO PLAY

Give a set of cards to each group. Ask one student from each group to shuffle them, then place them facedown on the table in five rows of four cards each. The first player turns over two cards and reads what is written on them. If the contents of both cards work together as one logical conditional sentence, that student can pick up those cards and go again. If the sentences do not work together as one logical conditional sentence, then that student must return the cards to the facedown position, and the next person can have a turn. Play continues until all of the cards have been matched. Keep in mind that depending on what conditional sentences you have written, there may be more than one match for an *if* clause. In that case, if the last two cards don't match, the player can win the point if he or she can make a logical statement using the *if* clause.

WHAT TO LOOK FOR

Make sure that the student whose turn it is reads the clauses written on the cards aloud and doesn't just play in silence.

To extend the game, have the groups take all the *if* clauses from their set of cards and write their own secondary clause to complete the sentence. For example, they could write, "If I were an animal, I would be a bird." This can be extended even further if the original sentences can be discussion starters. For example, another student might ask, "Why would you be a bird?"

96

Conditional Heads and Tails

★
LEVEL:
3 to 5

👤
GROUP:
WHOLE
CLASS

🕐
10
MINUTES

Additional Skills: Grammar (conditionals),
Listening, Speaking

MATERIALS & PREP WORK

None.

THE GAME

The object of the game is to provide a statement that connects to the previous player while using a conditional sentence. The game works best with the second conditional, but the first and third conditionals can be effective as well, depending on the level of your students.

HOW TO PLAY

This explanation presents the game as a whole-class activity, but you can divide the class in half if you have a large class. Before you begin, decide which conditional grammar you want to practice. Here is an example using the second conditional. Write the first half of an *if* clause sentence on the board, such as "If I were an animal ..." The first student completes the sentence like this: "If I were an animal, I would be an elephant." The next student continues by using the second clause of the sentence as his or her opening *if* clause: "If I were an elephant, I would eat peanuts." The third student continues in a similar way: "If I ate peanuts, I would get fat." The fourth student also continues in the same format: "If I got fat, I would buy a lot of new clothes." Play is finally over when a student can't produce a new sentence.

WHAT TO LOOK FOR

Make sure the students follow the pattern as described above. Each student needs to start his or her conditional sentence using the second half of the previous student's sentence. Note that the story line itself can change, as in the fourth student's example above, but the pattern of the story has to stay the same.

For higher-level students, you might require them to keep the story line restricted to the original subject. In this case, the fourth student would have had to say something relevant to an elephant because elephants can't "buy a lot of new clothes."

97

I Want to/ You Need to

LEVEL:
3 to 5

GROUP:
5 or 6

⏱
10 to 15
MINUTES

Additional Skills: Grammar (modals of necessity), Speaking, Listening

MATERIALS & PREP WORK

Provide a bell for each group.

THE GAME

The object of the game is for students to think and react quickly. One student will make a statement about something that he or she wants to do. Another student in the group then has to give him or her advice.

HOW TO PLAY

Give each group a bell. Write the following on the board: "I want to _____/You (have to) (need to) (should) _____." Model the activity by asking a student to complete the first sentence. The student might say, "I want to eat pizza." First, hit the bell, then say, "You should go to Mario's Pizza Shop.... I want to relax." Wait until you get a suggestion from someone who catches on. Then, play begins. In each group, one student goes first with "I want to ..." Someone else hits the bell when he or she has a response and the next prompt. For example, the first student says, "I want to see a movie." Another student says, "You need to go to the theater. I want to buy a car." Another student hits the bell and says, "You need to get a job and earn money."

WHAT TO LOOK FOR

Make sure the students are using a variety of modals, such as *should, must, need to,* and so on.

> You could have the students respond in order. If a student can't come up with a response, that player is out.

I'd Never!

Additional Skills: Grammar (modal verbs: would, could, might, may), Listening, Speaking

LEVEL:
3 to 5

GROUP:
WHOLE
CLASS

10 to 15
MINUTES

98

MATERIALS & PREP WORK

Prepare a list of oddball gifts that someone could possibly receive—for example, an ugly sweater, a door stopper, a plastic fish, slippers with mop pads on the bottom, etc. Do a Google Image search for "weird inventions" for ideas. Write the name of each item on a card, and make at least one card for each student in the class.

THE GAME

This game allows students to practice the target language by discussing what they would do if given an oddball gift for their birthday.

HOW TO PLAY

Write the modals on the board and, holding up a card or picture of one of the oddball gifts, ask the class, "What would you do if you got this [sweater, etc.] as a birthday gift?" Elicit some answers based on the modals. Then, hand one or two cards to each student and have a mixer. Students should go around the room asking, "What would you do if you got [a plastic fish] for your birthday present?" A classmate can answer, "I would hang it on the wall" or "I could put it on my desk," and so on. After a minute, change partners.

WHAT TO LOOK FOR

You can encourage the students to be creative with their answers. The target language used in their answers is what's most important.

Have the students write down each partner's answers and, at the end of the activity, share the most original or funniest response with the class.

99

Stopped "Doing" or Stopped "to Do"

LEVEL:
3 to 5

GROUP:
WHOLE
CLASS

10 to 15
MINUTES

Additional Skills: Grammar (stop followed by a gerund or an infinitive), Writing

MATERIALS & PREP WORK

Prepare a list of things you can stop "doing" (like stop smoking, stop working, etc.) and a list of things you can stop "to do" (like buy coffee, have lunch, etc.).

THE GAME

The object of this game is for students to use this grammar pattern properly in a sentence.

HOW TO PLAY

This is an activity appropriate for the end of a lesson when this grammar point has just been taught. Demonstrate the activity first. Call out a phrase and ask the students to try to make a sentence using that phrase, plus *stop*, plus the reason. For example, suggest "have lunch." A student creates a sentence: "I stopped to have lunch because I was hungry." (It would be incorrect to say "I stopped *having* lunch because I was hungry.") When the students
get the idea, you can start the activity by calling out another phrase from your list.

WHAT TO LOOK FOR

Since this is a whole class activity, tell the students they cannot answer twice in a row.

> You can also make this a writing activity. Instead of calling out the sentences, the students could write them down, then work in pairs to check their work.

What Would You Do?

100

Additional Skills: Grammar (second conditional), Listening, Speaking

LEVEL:
3 to 5

**GROUP:
WHOLE
CLASS**

🕐
10 to 15
MINUTES

MATERIALS & PREP WORK

Prepare cards proposing different scenarios in question form. Ask the questions using the second conditional, starting with "What would you do if … ?" A few examples might be "What would you do if you woke up in another person's house?" and "What would you do if you saw a UFO land close to the road where you were driving?" You will need at least one card for each student.

THE GAME

The object of this game is to practice using the second conditional in a natural, conversational way.

HOW TO PLAY

Hand out one or two cards to each student, and then ask the class to stand up and pick a partner. Tell the students to ask their partner the question on their card and then, depending on their partner's reply, to ask some follow-up questions. After two or three minutes, ask the pairs to exchange cards and then switch to another partner to repeat the activity. The idea here is that over the course of the game, the students will be asking and answering different questions about different topics while practicing the second conditional.

WHAT TO LOOK FOR

Make sure the students are using the second conditional in their answers.

You might vary this mixer as follows: After the first round, have the students tell their new partner what the previous partner said.

The Man Crosses the River

LEVEL:
3 to 5

GROUP:
3 or 4

10 to 15 MINUTES

Additional Skills: Grammar (conditionals)

MATERIALS & PREP WORK

Prepare a handout with the following old riddle on it: A man has a snake, a burger, and a mouse. He wants to bring all three to the other side of the river in his boat, but he can bring only one at a time. But if he takes the burger, the snake will eat the mouse. If he takes the snake, the mouse will eat the burger. How will he accomplish this task?

THE GAME

The object of the game is for students to solve the riddle.

HOW TO PLAY

This is an excellent activity for practicing the first and second conditionals. Hand out a copy of the worksheet to each student, and ask the class to read through it. Tell the students they will have 10 minutes to discuss it with their partners, then they will write down the solution and their reasoning. Remember, the key point here is tenses: Practice those conditionals. Students can appoint one group member to be the scribe, or they can each write the solution. Make it a game by giving a prize to the first group that completes the task.

WHAT TO LOOK FOR

Make sure the students are using the target language (conditionals) as they discuss the solution.

> You may want to limit the group to either the first or second conditional, depending on your class goals.

Solution to the Riddle:
The snake won't eat the burger, so he takes the mouse first. He then returns and puts the burger in the boat. When he gets to the other side, he leaves the burger and brings the mouse back to the original side. Then, he leaves the mouse and brings the snake across the river. Now, the snake and burger are on the other side. Finally, he goes back and picks up the mouse.

RESOURCES

Here are my recommendations for where you can find more supporting material for your classroom.

Practical English Usage by Michael Swan. This book is the bible for ESL teachers. There is no better resource for a clear explanation of grammar and vocabulary.

Jazz Chants by Carolyn Graham. This is an amazing series of books for practicing American English pronunciation and intonation.

Diary of a Wimpy Kid by Jeff Kinney. This is a great resource for everyday, real spoken English.

English the American Way by Sheila MacKechnie Murtha and Jane Airey O'Connor. This book has excellent idiom lessons based on American cultural themes.

Grammar in Use by Raymond Murphy. The best book for a one-point grammar lesson has a new version with North American English.

Google Images (images.Google.com). This is the best place to find the pictures and images mentioned in games here.

Longman Dictionary of Contemporary English Online (LDOCEonline.com). This is my go-to place for a clear definition and an example sentence.

Breaking News English (BreakingNewsEnglish.com). This site posts two or three lessons per week, mostly based on unique and offbeat news stories, that are excellent for classroom discussions.

American English (AmericanEnglish.state.gov) is a website from the State Department with lots of lessons related to American culture, holidays, and more.

Yarn! (GetYarn.io) is a website where you can search for a phrase and get clips from movies or TV shows cued up to that phrase.

Happy English (MyHappyEnglish.com) is my website, where you can find over 2,000 one-point English lessons for free.

CHOOSE A GAME

TITLE	★ LEVEL					🕐 MINUTES	👤 GROUP
1. Reply Relay	1	2	3			5–10	WHOLE
2. Giving Directions	1	2				10–15	2
3. Tongue Twister Chain	1	2	3	4	5	10–15	4–5
4. The Smartest Student		2	3	4		10–15	3–4
5. Chain Story		2	3	4		10–15	4
6. How Was Your Weekend?		2	3	4		10	2
7. Magazine Photos		2	3	4		10–15	5–6
8. Who Are We Talking About?		2	3	4		15–20	2
9. Two Numbers, Two Words		2	3	4	5	10–15	2–3
10. The Fastest Lyrics		2	3	4	5	10–15	2
11. A Dark & Stormy Night		2	3	4	5	10–15	3–4
12. Did You Say …?.		2	3	4	5	10–15	3–4
13. Dead Guy in the Hat			3	4	5	20–30	WHOLE
14. The Perfect New Roommate			3	4	5	20–25	WHOLE
15. Just One of the Actors			3	4	5	10–15	2

Speaking Games

Speaking Games

TITLE	LEVEL					MINUTES	GROUP
16. Survivor			3	4	5	15–20	3–4
17. Let's Take a Photo			3	4	5	10–15	4–5
18. A Night at the Improv			3	4	5	20–30	2
19. Video Dialogue			3	4	5	10–15	3–4
20. Wacky Debates			3	4	5	20–30	2–4
21. What's Missing?			3	4	5	15–20	2–4
22. Wild Conversation Starters			3	4	5	20–25	2
23. Time to Go	1	2				10–15	4–5
24. Going on a Picnic	1	2	3			10	5–6
25. Crazy Rhymes	1	2	3			10–15	3–4
26. Listening Cloze	1	2	3			10–15	2–3
27. What Am I Doing?		2	3	4		15–20	4–5
28. Find the Mistake Dictation		2	3	4		10–15	3–4
29. Police Sketch		2	3	4	5	10–15	4
30. Who Said That?		2	3	4	5	10	4–5
31. How's the Weather?			3	4	5	10–15	2
32. Card on the Head			3	4	5	15–20	4–5
33. Private Party			3	4	5	10–15	WHOLE
34. Truth or Lie			3	4	5	15–20	4–5
35. What Did You Catch?			3	4	5	10	3–4

Listening Games

TITLE	LEVEL					MINUTES	GROUP
36. What's the Question?	1	2	3	4		20–25	3
37. Picture Story		2	3	4	5	15–20	2–3
38. Two Truths, One Fib		2	3	4	5	10–15	2–4
39. Jungle Diaries			3	4	5	15–20	2–3
40. Rappin' ABCs			3	4	5	20–30	3–4
41. Seuss Tales			3	4	5	15–20	3–4
42. Stray Cat Strut			3	4	5	30	2
43. Weekday Update!			3	4	5	40–60	2
44. Weird Dreams			3	4	5	20–30	2–3
45. Broken Conversation	1	2	3	4		10–15	2–3
46. It's the Law		2	3	4	5	15–20	3–4
47. Why Did You Say That?		2	3	4	5	10–15	WHOLE
48. Mixed-Up Stories			3	4	5	10–15	3–4
49. Opposite Concentration	1	2	3			10–15	3
50. Picure-ary	1	2	3			10–15	WHOLE
51. Languages & Countries	1	2	3			10–15	3–4
52. Question Word Match	1	2	3			10–15	WHOLE
53. That's Not Regular: Singular or Plural?	1	2	3			10	2–3
54. Strange Stories	1	2	3			10–15	3–4
55. Phonics Drill	1	2	3	4		10–15	3–4

Writing & Reading Games

Vocabulary Games

TITLE			★ LEVEL			⏰ MINUTES	👤 GROUP

Vocabulary Games

TITLE			★ LEVEL			⏰ MINUTES	👤 GROUP
56. Best Match	1	2	3	4	5	10–15	3–4
57. Password	1	2	3	4	5	15–20	2
58. Crazy Descriptions		2	3	4		10–15	3–4
59. What's My Line?		2	3	4		20	4–5
60. Scattered Categories		2	3	4	5	10	3–4
61. Fancy Fairy Tales			3	4	5	20–30	3–4
62. Funniest Answer			3	4	5	15–20	4–5
63. My Secret			3	4	5	10–15	4–5
64. Question Me			3	4	5	10	4–5

Spelling & Number Games

TITLE			★ LEVEL			⏰ MINUTES	👤 GROUP
65. Did You Write It Right?	1	2	3			10–15	3–4
66. Word List Race	1	2	3			10–15	3–4
67. A Kind Elephant	1	2	3	4	5	10–15	3–4
68. First Two/Last Two	1	2	3	4	5	10–15	3–4
69. Silly Tongue Twisters		2	3	4	5	10–15	3–4
70. Prefix Opposites			3	4	5	10–15	3–4
71. Suffix Challenge			3	4	5	10	2–3
72. Say the Number	1	2	3			5–10	5–6
73. Big Number Bingo	1	2	3			10	2
74. Number Dictation	1	2	3			10–15	2–3
75. The Price Is Right	1	2	3			10–15	3–4
76. Did You Catch That?			3	4	5	10–15	3–4

TITLE	LEVEL					MINUTES	GROUP
77. The Great Adjective Divide	1	2	3			10–15	3–4
78. Get in Line	1	2	3			10–15	5–6
79. At, On, In	1	2	3			5–10	5–6
80. How's Your Memory?	1	2	3			10–15	2–3
81. Comparative Race	1	2	3			10–15	2–3
82. For or Since	1	2	3			10–15	WHOLE
83. It's Sporty	1	2	3			10–15	3
84. Make 'Em Say It	1	2	3			10–15	2
85. Not Regular Bingo	1	2	3			10–15	3–4
86. What Is/Was Going On?	1	2	3			10	2–3
87. An Educated Guess	1	2	3			5–15	5–10
88. Back to the Future		2	3	4		10–15	2–3
89. Because …		2	3	4		10–15	3–4
90. Draw the Scene		2	3	4		10–15	4–5
91. Future Me		2	3	4		10–15	WHOLE
92. Mixed-Up Schedules		2	3	4		10–15	WHOLE
93. An Old-Fashioned Postcard		2	3	4		10	2
94. Best Advice		2	3	4	5	10–15	4–5
95. Conditional Concentration		2	3	4	5	10–15	3–4

Grammar Games

	TITLE			LEVEL			MINUTES	GROUP
Grammar Games	**96.** Conditional Heads and Tails			3	4	5	10	WHOLE
	97. I Want to/You Need to			3	4	5	10−15	5−6
	98. I'd Never!			3	4	5	10−15	WHOLE
	99. Stopped "Doing" or Stopped "to Do"			3	4	5	10−15	WHOLE
	100. What Would You Do?			3	4	5	10−15	WHOLE
	101. The Man Crosses the River			3	4	5	10−15	3−4

ABOUT THE AUTHOR

MICHAEL DIGIACOMO started teaching English as a foreign language to adults at a private language school in Sendai, Japan, in 1994. He taught groups and private lessons there for four years and eventually became a new-teacher mentor. In 1998 he transferred to that company's school in New York City, where he worked as a teacher and program coordinator. He worked his way up the corporate ladder in that school until 2010, when he formed Happy English, his own ESL tutoring company in New York. He teaches private lessons, does a podcast, and has a YouTube channel to help students all over the world learn English.

CPSIA information can be obtained
at www.ICGtesting.com
Printed in the USA
BVHW010313180723
667393BV00004B/28

9 781641 521093